Acclaim for Ana Veciana-Suarez and her debut novel,
The Chin Kiss King

"As sweet and tart as the tropical fruits that are savored by
the ebullient trio of Cuban-American women at its heart . . .
wise and touching."

—*The New York Times Book Review*

"Deeply touching. An important addition to the literary
tradition of Cuba . . . vivid and emotionally charged.
Veciana-Suarez has created characters who are tender,
compassionate, and often illuminating. She has written an
engaging and memorable novel . . . A powerful and
haunting story of the world of our spirits and spirituality . . .
bewitching for its lyricism and for its evocative powers."

—*The Boston Globe*

"An amazing grace of a debut novel. Bravely, with poetic
vibrancy and insight, fierce tenderness, bits of magic up her
sleeves, and lusty humor, Veciana-Suarez orchestrates a
poignant tale of how ordinary people are transformed and
enlightened by heartbreak. This is the truest book about
maternal fortitude and devotion that I have ever read, one
that deserves celebration."

—*Raleigh News & Observer*

"In the tradition of Julia Alvarez's *How the Garcia Girls Lost
Their Accents* and Cristina Garcia's *Dreaming in Cuban* . . .
Beautifully written . . . introduces a narrative voice that is
sure, wickedly omniscient, and very strong."

—*St. Petersburg Times*

Ana Veciana-Suarez is a popular syndicated columnist based
at *The Miami Herald*, and the author of the acclaimed novel
The Chin Kiss King (available in a Plume edition). Born in
Cuba, she lives in Florida with her family.

"A remarkable novel. Emotionally resonant, full of life,
finally redemptive. . . . A vital sense of place and the
neighborhood of idiom is at work here, as well as a sly sense
of humor."
                    —*The Star-Ledger* (Newark, New Jersey)

"Captures the reader's heart with its compassion for family
feeling, personal crisis, and cultural heritage."
                              —*Richmond Times-Dispatch*

"Suarez's combination of lyrical power and frank storytelling
make *The Chin Kiss King* a heartfelt debut."
                                    —*The Hartford Courant*

"Veciana-Suarez writes eloquently . . . A true gift to her
readers. [*The Chin Kiss King*] is poignant, enlightening,
moving, thought-provoking, and . . . humorous."
                              —*The Orlando Sunday Sentinel*

"There is a fierce, feminine magic between the covers of *The
Chin Kiss King*. Veciana-Suarez's prose will make you jealous
of those who live in her peculiar, abundant, sensual world."
                                    —*The Grand Rapids Press*

"*The Chin Kiss King* is a timeless, captivating story."
                                          —*Vibe* magazine

Birthday Parties in Heaven

Thoughts on Love, Life, Grief, and Other Matters of the Heart

Ana Veciana-Suarez

A PLUME BOOK

PLUME
Published by the Penguin Group
Penguin Putnam Inc., 375 Hudson Street,
New York, New York 10014, U.S.A.
Penguin Books Ltd, 27 Wrights Lane,
London W8 5TZ, England
Penguin Books Australia Ltd, Ringwood,
Victoria, Australia
Penguin Books Canada Ltd, 10 Alcorn Avenue,
Toronto, Ontario, Canada M4V 3B2
Penguin Books (N.Z.) Ltd, 182–190 Wairau Road,
Auckland 10, New Zealand

Penguin Books Ltd, Registered Offices:
Harmondsworth, Middlesex, England

First published by Plume,
a member of Penguin Putnam Inc.

First Printing, October 2000
10 9 8 7 6 5 4 3 2 1

 REGISTERED TRADEMARK—MARCA REGISTRADA

CIP data is available.
ISBN 0-452-28200-4

Printed in the United States of America
Set in Simoncini Garamond Roman
Designed by Leonard Telesca

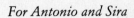

For Antonio and Sira

ACKNOWLEDGMENTS

My thanks to Ileana Oroza, whose helpful suggestions improved every essay, and to Fran Collin and Rosemary Ahern, who believed in this book before I did. And thanks, too, to my husband, David Freundlich, whose love, encouragement, and unwavering support made the writing possible.

Contents

Birthday Parties
in Heaven

My Lowly
Thatched Cottage

When David goes back to the house he hasn't sold, the home he occupied and decorated for ten years before we met, he collapses in the master bedroom's bed and squirms and sniffs like a puppy that has returned, finally, to the warmth of its litter. "Aah," he sighs. "Oooh!" he coos. The look of pleasure is so genuine, so heartfelt, that my insecurities gradually vanish. This is not a reflection of our relationship, I tell myself, or of the home we are trying to build together. It is merely the expression of comfort at its safest and most familiar, like that soothing relief we feel when, after a long trip, we return to the well-known contours of our bed.

I have watched David amble about his house with a sense of ownership he does not display anywhere else. He turns on the light switches without patting the wall. He opens the front door without rifling through the set of keys. He goes to the bathroom in the middle of the night without bothering to turn on the light. And he does it all with the ease of practice and the power of experience. To a degree, he does the same in our home—Ana's house, as he sometimes calls it—but I think his actions there carry a measure of reserve. He still feels that most things (curtains, fans, cabinets, doors) are not his, not yet at least. And I can't say I blame him. Familiarity doesn't come quickly or easily, or at least it shouldn't. It takes time, both in number of days and quality of hours, for us to assume intimacy with something.

"I know where everything is," he tells me, during the parade through his bedrooms, baths, and kitchen. "All I have to do is reach out and touch it."

Reach out and touch it: so important this tactile perception of home.

He also announces the obvious as if it were the first time he is saying it: "I love this house!"

Before we married and for a few months thereafter, we discussed selling his property. There was never a question of where we would live because most homes, including his, aren't big enough to accommodate a brood of five kids and the trail of toys, clothes, shoes, books, magazines, sports trophies, framed photos, and just plain ol' junk that accompanies such a crowd. Besides, stability for the children was high on my list in a remarriage. Our idea was to eventually, once my older children were on their own, sell my house and buy an "our" house, a compromise of place and situation. Things haven't quite worked out the way we thought, however. A soft real estate market in his part of town dissuaded us from putting up a For Sale sign, and so his house sits without occupant twenty-one miles away from mine, a reminder that attempts to build a nest, twig by twig, string by string, are too often complicated by things out of our control.

David's place, still furnished, still operational with all its utilities, has gotten me thinking about what makes a house a home, and how, even when we become accustomed to our surroundings for the sake of love and peace, we can still feel like exiles in the place where we reside. Home is never as sweet and peaceful as when we leave it. I am the daughter of exiles, and so know of what I speak. I am familiar with the subtle pangs of nostalgia and the more virulent waves of homesickness. I know that what you don't have, what you give up, becomes better with time and distance. Faults are forgotten, blemishes erased.

That's not to say David's house isn't a wonderful place on its own merits. Patterned after old Conch houses in the Keys, it sits on massive concrete columns overlooking leafy treetops, an octagonal-shaped home of gray-tile floors, yawning spaces, vast closets, and wide windows. It is replete with bittersweet memories of triumph and tragedy. This is the house that sweat and determination and his own hands built. He began life there alone with his children after his first marriage ended, and he rebuilt it after Hurricane Andrew used it as a giant food processor in 1992. No wonder that something with so much history and symbolism is difficult to forget.

I, too, like it, like its simplicity and charm, and have, in the past few months, spent more time in it than he has. Twice a week, sometimes more often, I drive southwest, from the manicured rigidity of my walled upperclass subdivision to the rambling, weedy, buggy groves and farms of rural Miami-Dade County. Dodging tractors and produce trucks, I speed down a paved thoroughfare until I turn onto a dirt road, where homes of different sizes and pretensions interrupt the hues of waxy green, mottled brown, and blue the shade of stonewashed jeans. His house of weathered wood is set back from the road, peeking out on five acres of exotic tropical fruit: lychees, longans, pomelos, mamey, sour oranges.

This is where I come to write.

Sometimes, though, I just sit. From the kitchen table, or the living-room sofa, I watch this foreign world with a mix of awe and apprehension. Crows pick at ripening fruit. A jackrabbit hops onto an open field, turns to look both ways, then hops back into the undergrowth. A cardinal or two, maybe three, fly in a flash of red from tree to bush to nest. Across the road, a brown cow munches on the grass, chewing ever so patiently while a white cattle egret balances itself on its meaty hump. When it's cooler, I open the windows and listen to the strange noises: the chirp of a jay, the haunting call of a whippoorwill, the metallic gurgle of an irrigation pump at work. In the afternoons, if I'm attentive, I can smell the rain coming in.

Still, for all the sensuality of the country, I feel like an alien there.

I'm a city girl, born and bred. When we stay overnight, sleeping co-
zily in the bed David so likes, in the house he so misses, I am occasionally frightened by the denseness of the country night.

"It's so dark here," I complain.

"Yeah," he agrees, smiling, "and look at the stars."

Ah, the stars, so many, so bright, some I never even knew were
up there.

It occurs to me that these day trips into a world I knew little
about until I met David are a form of exile, self-imposed and temporary of course, but a separation from the known nonetheless.
The temporary quality is what, to some extent, defines exile, what
differentiates this process from that of immigration. An exile ex-
pects to return as soon as a government falls. He cannot imagine it
any other way.

Though I am in the grove house provisionally, I have tried to
mark it with something of my own, in much the same way students
decorate their hallway lockers: to stake a claim for a while. I crave
possessions, things that belong to me as surely as I belong to them.
So over time I have transported from one house to another two potted African violets, still without bloom, one cordless telephone,
snacks for the refrigerator, magazines for writer's block, framed
photographs, and a wedding gift I didn't know what else to do
with. These "flags" are strategically placed so I can see them when
I look up from the tyranny of my computer screen.

When I was young, my parents did the same in our first houses
in exile. What they had managed to squirrel out of Cuba—a black-
and-white wedding photograph, say, or a small, carved jewelry
box—was given prominent display. Or they improvised. To this day
my favorite wall hangings are the tacky calendars advertising a
mom-and-pop bodega or a neighborhood *farmacía* while reminding
loyal customers of home with pictures of Cuba's natural wonders
and historical sites.

The other night I asked David if he was ever going to sell the
grove. He had mentioned earlier in the week that a couple of homes
in the area had already sold.

"As a matter of fact . . ." he replied, and I wondered if I wasn't asking him to give up too much.

The Bible's book of Jeremiah traces the fall of Jerusalem, the destruction of the city and the Temple, and the exile to Babylonia of Judah's king and many of his people. At the end, it precisely tallies the numbers: 3,023 people in the seventh year, 832 in the eighteenth year, 745 in the twenty-third year—in all, 4,600 exiles. You would think that the people of Judah would have gotten the hang of exile by then. After all, their ancestors had wandered in the wilderness for forty years, after they had left Egypt and before homesteading in the Promised Land. Yet, an entire book, Lamentations, is devoted to the aftermath of ruin and exile that followed the destruction of Jerusalem in 586 B.C.

The old people no longer sit at
the city gate,
and the young people no
longer make music.

Happiness has gone out of our
lives;
grief has taken the place of
our dances.

When the Jewish exiles fled to the Chebar River in Babylonia, and when Moses' Israelites trudged through Moab and Kadesh Barnea, when they crossed the Jordan and camped near the Gulf of Suez, how did they think of home? In what way did they make desert and riverland a familiar, if not welcoming, domicile? Did they carry a potted houseplant from one encampment to the next? Was the carved chair, a family heirloom, given prominent display under the tent? Did they cook food in the same way with the same pots and the same tools? How did they realize they had arrived where they belonged? Was it the certainty of knowing where everything is? The feelings of welcome and repose? Or was it simply arbitrary boundaries drawn from here to there by an alternately loving and wrathful God?

My parents have been exiles for an almost biblical forty years, and though they have not wandered in the physical wilderness like the Israelites, they have known, at least in the beginning, a spiritual wasteland of sorts: the isolation of not belonging, the harshness of the unfamiliar. Their Jerusalem floated one-hundred-and-forty miles from where they live today. It was a paradise of halcyon nights and glorious days, an island where the ocean was bluer, the sand whiter, the palms taller. It never existed, of course. Nostalgia rewrites history. Yet my parents would have given anything over the years to return to Cuba, to live again in Havana's La Vibora neighborhood, in their little tiled house with the wrought-iron, gated porch; to walk the little narrow streets that weren't always clean; and to shop in their little bodegas that weren't always well stocked but where everybody knew their names. (Nineteenth-century American playwright John Howard Payne hit the nail on the head when he wrote in "Home Sweet Home," from the opera *Clari, the Maid of Milan*: "An exile from home splendor dazzles in vain, / Oh give me my lowly thatched cottage again. . . .") Instead of the tiny home in La Vibora, it was *el exilio*—a state of limbo when you are where you don't expect to be—that defined the final years of my parents' youth and all of their middle age. It marked my childhood, too.

We did not celebrate Thanksgiving, the most American of holidays, until my last years in elementary school. I have no early memories of pumpkin pie and sweet potato casseroles, of family gathered around the bounty of a table. Unless it was Christmas Eve. And even then, Christmas was a subdued affair, with none of the overwrought glitz of today. We did not get a Christmas tree until I was in fourth or fifth grade, a fake silver beauty that I watched for hours on end when the revolving colors of a reflector light shone on it. This penury during the holidays, I now believe, had little to do with money but plenty to do with hope—hope that life in these United States would be temporary, hope that next Christmas would be celebrated in Havana, hope that one day they would look back at this period of their lives as something sad but brief, and altogether finished. Celebrating would have been to admit a hopelessness. This is how exile translates into marginality, a living on the sidelines without knowing when to jump into the game.

Yet, little by little, first in word then by action, whether they knew it or not, their lives evolved into a search for rootedness. My parents bought a house when they had saved up enough money and explained it this way: Very few people would rent out to foreigners with young children, even if these renters were clean, modestly dressed, well-mannered, and professionals in another country. Eventually they fixed up this house, added a bathroom and bedroom for the in-laws, put up a fence, remodeled the kitchen, planted a mango tree in the back and red ixora bushes in the front. As their children grew older, as their children birthed children in exile, they spoke less of a return to Cuba—"When we go back home . . ."—and more of the horrible possibility that, in their old age, they would be put in a nursing home in much the same way that *los americanos* sent their old folk away. My mother talked about retiring to a condo in Miami Beach; my father spoke of expanding the business.

When did exile become home? After they planted the mango? When the grandchildren were born? Now, as they approach retirement?

I have grown interested in answers as I see David wandering about my house, or collapsing in his old bed in his old house in the grove. No matter what he says, I know he doesn't feel at home in either place. He is where my parents were about twenty years ago—in between, not there but not quite here either.

My family has lived in three different countries and spoken three different languages in the span of three generations. My grandparents, Catalonians on both sides, fled their homeland because of poverty and civil war. Their foods and their language, that rich guttural Catalan I heard in my childhood, eventually melded with the new customs of their new island home. Their children, in turn, later scrambled across the Florida Straits to another exile, also because of political upheaval. What, I sometimes wonder, might be in store for me? As a woman listening to stories of my ancestors' comings and goings, as a Catholic married to a Jew who has never seen his people's Promised Land, the concept of home is important to me. But not only to me—actually to most everybody I know. We all need a place where we belong, a place to return to, where the contours of the bed are well-known and the light switches are just where they're supposed to be: a place where we can listen quietly, comfortably, to the stirrings of the heart and whispers of the soul.

My Father, *Mi Papi*

For a good part of my childhood, I remained convinced that all fathers, while working, smelled of chalk and mildew—a scent that was as strong as it was strangely sweet when it permeated a room, entered the nostrils, and finally homesteaded there. It is perhaps one of my most enduring memories of Papi, this smell, and it is also probably the most untrustworthy one. Memory deceives, distills, defines, and, yes, sometimes it cheats. I cling to it, however, because it is something to hold on to, something tangible and at least partly true.

When I was a child, Papi and his friends met regularly in a rented storefront in Allapattah, a Miami neighborhood where the whites were fleeing the incoming Cubans and the native blacks, a neighborhood in transition, like the exiled revolutionaries who came. The store was not far from Jackson High School and a stone's throw from an ice cream shop, which we visited often because back then a single scoop wouldn't break your piggy bank. This storefront was where I learned to read Spanish, where I first memorized the verses of Cuban poet José Martí, and where I learned the geography and history of my Caribbean homeland from the wives of men who wanted to liberate the island through war.

This was also where my father kept his guns.

Now he says he didn't. But fact plays no part in my story. Truth, my memory of it, is more important. If he and the anti-Communist commando group he helped found did not keep guns, they kept something just as powerful: passion and righteousness.

I cannot remember much else about the storefront, or what was in it. Except, of course, the chalk, because the mothers needed it to teach us and because the men used it, too, to plot whatever it was they plotted on the blackboard. Perhaps there was a map of Cuba taped to the wall, and alongside it a color rendition of its flag and a pencil sketch of Martí the Liberator, complete with bushy moustache and wide forehead. There may have been photographs of the oceanfront Malecón and the Cuban Capitol, of a peasant's thatched-roof bohío, of El Morro Castle and numerous other scenes of a country my six-year-old mind was quickly and inevitably forgetting.

But maybe not. Perhaps the walls were left blank, a surrender to peeling paint and rusty nails. I'm not sure. Sometimes I wonder why I even want to know.

I loved going there. I loved the way the mothers wrote lessons on a large portable chalkboard, with efficient, elegant handwriting and yellow chalk that dusted our clothes. I loved the way we started class, with the U.S. Pledge of Allegiance and the Cuban National Anthem. I loved the soft, melodious sound of children's voices reading their Spanish: *Mamá bebe agua. José bebe leche. ¿Qué bebe el bebé?* I loved straining to listen to my father's muffled voice in the other room, using his own chalk and blackboard, and to feel the important bustling of busy men who sometimes argued so loudly that we could not hear our teachers above their din. I loved, too, the pastries at midmorning because the guava was always warm and the crust flaky. It did not matter if summer rains gave this storefront a perpetual smell of mildew that stuck to our skin. Nor was it important that most other children I knew spent Saturday mornings watching cartoons.

It didn't matter because my Papi was there.

One year, we children staged a show of Cuban folkloric dance and song with the help of the women and the encouragement of the men. For my number, I wore skin-colored tights, T-strap black shoes, and a dress my mother had sewed: a white, frilly country gown with red satin ribbons at the cinched waist and scooped neckline. Mami painted my lips the color of cherry and circled my eyes in blue. With a black pencil she darkened my eyebrows and rubbed a beauty mark near my mouth. Standing beside my dance partner, the white-shirted, straw-hatted, red-kerchiefed older brother, I was immortalized in this flouncy outfit by a family photographer, probably my father. I keep this photograph in an old scrapbook, proof that I danced the *zapateo* on a well-lighted stage. But I have no other confirmation except a deceiving memory to recall the initial vertigo of stage fright and that awful moment after the dance when, panicked by applause, I froze in the lights and refused to disappear behind the curtains until my father called for me.

Never happened, he tells me. I danced without misstep or fault.

Over the years we participated in many outdoor events as well. Namely, we marched. A lot. On these parades, the men led us through Miami streets and over bridges, past gaping motorists and pedestrians, all of us walking proudly, walking defiantly, waving the Cuban flag and singing, a veritable conga line of politics and purpose. *Al combate corred bayameses que la patria os contempla orgullosa. . . .* I try to sing the anthem now, a melody that echoes in my head, but I stumble over the words. How long ago this must have been!

So, yes, we marched and we walked and we skipped, the women and children behind the men, until we arrived at Bayfront Park or the Cuban Refugee Center or some other important place of commerce that has long since been razed and redeveloped. Once there, one of the men, often my father, would roar words of justice, and his voice would rock the ground and move the women to tears, and we, the children of revolutionaries, thirsty, sweaty, and eager to play among our own, stood restless at attention by our mothers' sides for fear of getting smacked. It was always hot on those marches, and my thighs chafed and the men got dark rings of sweat under their arms and the women's dresses stuck to their backs. Police escorted us everywhere, usually on motorcycles, which thrilled the children in a way few things could. Sometimes the cops who led us rode on large brown horses, and because we behaved, our mothers allowed us to pet their manes.

The speeches, I don't remember what they were about, but they always finished with the hopeful shouts of *¡Viva Cuba Libra!,* shouts I recognize now as plaintive cries of dreams broken and promises disavowed. They ended, too, these marches, with everyone rushing the speaker to reach for that voice of confidence and authority. Entranced, bewildered, and jealous in a way I could not explain, I watched these people, their tangle of arms, their all-too visible hopes, and knew they possessed my father in a way I never could. I was simply a little girl, powerless and shy, and all I could offer was to adore him from afar.

My father doesn't deliver speeches anymore. The last time he spoke in public was in an auditorium where I was reading from my first novel. I recognized him in the audience and introduced him. Graciously he declared, "She used to be my daughter. Now I am her father."

We did not take many vacations when I was a child, but the few we did were memorable and exciting. One in particular, across the heart of South America, comes to mind. This is how I remember it:

The road ended abruptly and without explanation at the banks of a clear, cold river. Papi stopped the four-door blue sedan, which he had borrowed for our vacation, opened his door, and trudged to the river's edge. I watched from the backseat, feeling that too-familiar wave of anxiety ebbing in. We were traveling from Bolivia, through Peru, and into Chile. If roads in this part of the world are bad now, they were dismal then, pockmarked with craters if they were paved, and dirt and rock if one was lucky, or, during the rainy season, mud and puddles. Now we had run out of luck, and there was not even a recognizable path across.

Papi ordered us out of the car and sent us looking for shallows. My older brother, fifteen at the time, found it near a footbridge the Indians had built. We drove to the spot. In the distance, across the potato farms of the altiplano, I noticed how the Quechuas stopped their tilling to watch the white city folk cross their bridge. We carried bundles of clothes and heavy boxes. Then my father sped the car across the gurgling waters and met us on the other side. The wind was harsh, like a scorned lover's slap, and the landscape brown and desolate except for scrub and potato plants.

That was just the beginning of fun.

Later, in Peru, on a winding mountain road that descended into a village of some renown (it appeared, at least, on a map), the car wheezed, sputtered, coughed, then began to smoke. Nearing town it gave out completely, and we climbed out to push. Because it was Sunday, my father had to pay an exorbitant price—months' worth of wages in those parts—to find us lodging, food, and auto parts.

Undaunted, we continued south on the spine of the Andes. Two days later we crossed into Chile. Guards stopped us at the border and would not let us pass. My mother and the three children were given the run of a room. Somebody brought us sandwiches, soft drinks. We played, we must have. And, I'm sure, we fought. My father was gone for hours, sequestered in a room, I was told, getting our documents in order. It was nightfall before we saw him again. I don't remember the expression on his face, though I imagine now that it must have been ashen and preoccupied. I do remember thinking, with my child's logic, that my family had the most adventurous holidays of any family I knew.

Our vacation in Santiago, a cosmopolitan city with some of the best food I have ever eaten, coincided with Fidel Castro's 1971 visit to the then-Communist-controlled Chile. Under the seats of the blue sedan my father drove—the car that had forded a river, that had motored some of the steepest roads imaginable, that had conked out in the middle of nowhere, that actually belonged to the United States Government—somewhere in the bowels of that car a rifle and ammunition were stored. We sat on these valuables, my older brother, my younger sister, and I, singing "One hundred bottles of beer on the wall."

In September 1979, I was twenty-two years old and a year and a half out of college when my father was shot in the head. He was driving home from work at the family marine store, his regular route, when the driver of a brown Buick station wagon pulled alongside him and fired four shots. Blood spurted onto Papi's clothes, over the dashboard and steering wheel. Shaking and disoriented, he drove home, stumbled into the house where my two youngest siblings were playing, and collapsed in the living room.

I was working as a reporter at the time and had just returned from an assignment when one of the other city-desk writers, covering my father's shooting, pulled me aside and told me about it. My knees buckled.

Papi underwent surgery and was sent home from the hospital two days after the shooting. Miraculously, only one small-caliber bullet had lodged just above his ear. The others had dented the car or ricocheted off. Despite several leads, police never found the gunman, and the assassination attempt was attributed to "political circumstances." Several months before, the FBI had warned him about the possibility of an attempt on his life.

Following the incident, an editor asked me to write about my experience with political violence. My father's shooting had come on the heels of the assassination of another exile leader, this one in Puerto Rico. I wrote. Now, two decades later, I cannot remember a single line in that article, but that dry-mouth sensation when my colleague delivered the news remains vivid, a reminder of that oh-God-what-now? feeling that was as much a part of my childhood as squabbles with my sister and cold watermelon in the summer.

An accountant by trade and a revolutionary by vocation, Papi worked at different jobs when I was growing up. For a very long time, he was a boxing promoter, then a promoter of dance shows. In Bolivia, where we lived for four years, he returned to the profession he had practiced in Cuba—banking expert—but that turned out to be a brief sojourn. Regardless of what he did or where we lived, he was always involved in some shape or form with anti-Castro groups.

His parents were Catalonians, poor peasant stock with a knack for hard work and a spirit of sacrifice that have served me, two generations removed, in good stead. Though an only child, he grew up in a large, raucous house in Havana, with aunts and uncles and cousins and grandparents, a place everyone of that generation called *La Finca,* The Farm, a name he would later give another home in exile. He was brilliant and bookish as a child, a baseball fanatic of the most virulent kind, and spoiled by a mother who personally cut his steak well into his adolescence. (She, of course, ate whatever the butcher was throwing away.) He grew tall and lanky, traits I inherited from him, a serious man with deep-set eyes, an aquiline nose, and a large mole over his lips that he hid as soon as he could grow a moustache.

He is still brilliant, still a baseball fanatic, but no longer lanky. He has filled out with age, and sometimes he stoops. My children, his grandchildren, tease him about his choice of clothes. At home, he prefers colorful plaid shirts, Bermuda shorts, and black over-the-calf socks. His legs are as white as a Canadian tourist's, and he always manages to appear a bit disheveled, despite my mother's valiant attempts to improve his looks. He forgets to zip his fly sometimes, his shirttail scoots out, and his hair tends to stick up every which way. He has a sweet tooth of the worst sort.

He tends toward sentimentality. I can recall, on the fingers of one hand, the times I've seen my mother cry. I've lost count with my father. His eyes water in joy, in sadness, in resignation. This is not a man from the old school of machismo, a patriarch absent of emotions, mythological in his aloofness.

And yet . . . and yet. As a child, I felt my father more as presence than physical reality. He seemed to always be away, for work or for *la revolución,* busy doing things I could not understand or that were rarely talked about. He was a phantom, a mirage, a hologram.

I must often ask myself how much I truly remember about those years, and how much is imagination eager to fill in the blanks. I love to look at photographs of that time in my childhood, probably in hopes of recapturing what I could not possibly remember—what I may never have had and so might have made up.

In a worn, green scrapbook, there is a photo of the young refugee family, a black-and-white taken in January 1963 in front of the rock fireplace in the ramshackle house we lived in when we first arrived from Cuba. My mother looks heartbreakingly young, her face un-lined, her lips thick and smiling. My father wears baggy pants, and his hair, raven black and full, is cropped close. I can't tell if he's smiling. The three oldest children are in the foreground in donated clothes, pretty clothes, mind you. I am at my father's side; he is ca-ressing my cheek. Behind us, on the mantel, are the Cuban and American flags.

Another snapshot, June 1963: in the front yard of the same house in our Sunday finery. My brother wears a plaid jacket, my sister and I have matching purses and hats. Of course, I pose next to my fa-ther, his arm around my shoulder.

June 1980, color photograph: My father, in a gray tux, walks me down the church aisle to the muted strains of a wedding march. I have acquired curves, but in his eyes I'm still a child. His hair is graying on the sides. The photographer captures our smiles but not our words or emotions. My father's arm shakes, tears roll down his cheeks. "Will you calm down?" I whisper hoarsely.

Papi was not a roll-up-his-sleeves kind of father. He did not change diapers, give baths, or sing lullabies. He neither helped us learn our multiplication tables nor taught us to play ball. He never roughhoused with me, and if he did so with my brothers, I cannot remember, though my youngest sister, sixteen years my junior and the youngest of five, insists our father told her elaborate bedtime stories about a comical cow. I was out of the house by then, in col-lege first, then married.

My father rarely disciplined us, and that, I am sure, was part of his charm for us as children. My mother wielded a mean belt, and she was quick to pinch. Later, much later in life, when the father of my own children left the dispensing of privileges and punishments to me, I was bitterly resentful. Disneyland Dad, I called my husband, for he was the one associated with fun, and I with routine and wrath. Our good cop–bad cop routine, however, helped me understand my mother and my father and how they had chosen, maybe unconsciously, the disciplinary roles they would play in raising us.

I was a child known as much for my rages as for my quiet stubbornness. *Fosforito,* they called me during adolescence. Little match. I was fifteen the only time my father hit me. We had had an argument at the table. He wanted me to do something; I refused. I ran into my bedroom and locked it. He pounded on the door. As he picked the lock, I climbed onto the windowsill. From the second story, it was not a bad jump to the garden. We had tried it before, my middle sister and I, but somehow this time . . . this time. The hesitation cost me. He grabbed me by the hair and pulled me down. He slapped me. When we calmed down, he lectured then apologized for striking me. I turned my face away. I wouldn't talk to him for days. I wonder now who punished whom.

I'm sure he was reluctant to spend the little time he had with us in forcing us to do things we did not want to do. On the rare occasions he was home, when he was not at the chalky, mildewy Allapattah storefront or at the various jobs he held during those first years of exile (always abroad with revolutionary causes or show promotions), it was Christmas, New Year's, and the end of school all rolled into one. As the oldest daughter and the most verbal of his children, I was allowed to tag along with him wherever he went, to stores, to offices, to government agencies, wherever I could. I learned to blend in, to not speak loudly, certainly not unless I was spoken to, and to observe. I translated when journalists interviewed him about Cuban exile politics and when investigators from the House Select Committee on Assassinations initially contacted him to find out what he knew about John F. Kennedy's murder. (He eventually told the committee that, in 1963, through a CIA contact, he had met Lee Harvey Oswald in Dallas three months before Kennedy was killed there.)

As I matured, I began to witness my father's growing frustration with *la lucha,* the struggle for a free Cuba, and his bewilderment over a misguided perception others had about those who fought against Castro as right-wing thugs. He learned, as I did, that the printed word, the filmed image, and the broadcast voice can be as far from reality as a cartoon show. Because of him, I became a woman with sharply defined political ideas, liberal values that are also deeply held. Because of him, I refuse to discuss them aloud, however. In fact, I'm allergic to public discussion of politics of any kind. I learned very early on that arguing politics is as useless as describing color to the blind. We believe what we want to believe, regardless of the facts. Why waste time in talk?

But my father influenced more than political thought. What he is, what he would have hoped to be, has defined me as much as my own dreams. I, for example, owe my work habits to Papi. I have yet to meet anyone who works harder and longer and with as much passion. He always carries a file of some sort with him, or a stack of important-looking papers. Not in a briefcase, no, but bound together with a rubber band or secured in a plastic bag: notes, budgets, receipts, letters, outlines. Many of those sheets bear his loopy writing that is more flourish than practical. He refuses to retire, and I wonder if he enjoys running a business so much that he cannot imagine staying at home—or if he is afraid of what comes in old age, the time of questioning, the inevitable knowing of what might have been but wasn't.

As the first man I loved, he has, in one way or another, been a template for all the relationships that followed him. He taught me that virility and nurturing are not mutually exclusive and that the complicated matters of love can bring joy as well as pain, disillusion along with hope. And so I have had good luck in the affairs of the heart. I have loved and been loved passionately. I've always expected to be pampered, to be doted on, to be admired—but also to be respected and encouraged. For a Latino man, my father was—and still is—incredibly ambitious for his three daughters. He has pushed us to strive, to be at the top of our class, to be the best at our careers. We are all well-educated professionals, all women with minds of our own. Though my mother was very much of her generation and her culture—in other words, she knew her place, next to her husband—I was never raised to be somebody's wife. I was expected to be somebody in my own right. This was considered revolutionary thinking in his time.

Still, I tend to be inexplicably anxious about what he will think. So much of my life has been spent in an effort to not disappoint him. Not because of fear that I would not make the cut in his eyes. I could, and did, measure up. But because I needed to be better than he expected, better than my siblings, the outstanding among the extraordinary, the one he would notice in whatever way I could manage to get noticed. It wasn't, and isn't, enough to succeed in the public arena. A triumph doesn't count unless he witnesses it, unless I tell him about it.

Papi became gravely ill in 1993, when I was pregnant with my last child. After emergency open-heart surgery, he blinked awake in the recovery room and asked the nurse for his wallet. Barely conscious, barely able to move, he wanted to show her a letter to the editor that had recently appeared in *The Miami Herald* about my writing. My younger brother, who discovered this scene, described it so many times that its retelling was enough to cheer my father, to keep him motivated for months. The story, with embellishments and a little editing, underscored the nature of our relationship—a relationship I once described to my second husband as: "I'm the son he's always wanted."

That hospital stay marked a beginning and an end—a changing of the guard, if you will. Not long ago, driving out of a parking lot, my father blacked out at the wheel and smashed into another car. When I saw him shaken but unharmed at home, I recognized that vulnerability I had first seen at the hospital years earlier, after bypass surgery. There was something more, too—a softening of the features, the acceptance that suffuses us when we come to terms with our own faults and frailties. Inevitable, some might say, that I am parenting him more and he fathering me less.

The more successful I become, the more I learn about the world, and the farther I venture, the less it seems I need him. But I wonder about that. The ties that bind aging parent to adult child are like an elastic, ready to be stretched and tested before returning to form. I've been known to snap that elastic a few times.

When my first husband died suddenly of a heart attack at thirty-seven, leaving me with five children, the devastating loss gave my father a renewed purpose in life. He is, if anything, a man for impossible missions, and he felt I needed to be rescued.

Mi palomita herida, he called me. My injured dove.

He held me tight, oh yes, he did, sometimes with a suffocating grip. I thought he was making up for lost time, for all those childhood moments he had missed. Now I know different. Now I know that it was difficult, as well as painful, for him to watch me struggle alone through grief. He could not abide his own helplessness. So we argued about my decision to continue living alone with the children. We argued about money, career moves, new interests, and eventually new relationships. Suddenly, I was seventeen all over again.

Yet, the death of my children's Papi helped me view my own father with compassion and forgiveness. My children, left fatherless too soon, idolize their daddy, much the same way I adored mine as a little girl: from afar. But mine does not remain frozen in time, a perpetual thirty-seven-year-old, and I must be ever thankful for that. As I age, that once unreachable hero has taken human form, become a man like other men, with annoying habits and inexplicable idiosyncrasies, virtues, too, all real, all tangible and true. He no longer smells of chalk or mildew. Maybe he never did. His scent is of musky aftershave, sometimes of the seasoning in my mother's black beans.

The other night he phoned to complain that we had not spoken in two days. I chided him for whining, explained about deadlines, children's practices, church commitments, household duties: excuses he did not accept.

"*Pío, pío, pío,*" he joked before hanging up. "*La palomita vuela.*" The little dove flies.

I swear I detected a note of pride.

Stitchwork

After dinner, after the flurry of bedtime prayers and last-minute runs to the potty, my mother always settled by the yellow light of an ugly ceramic lamp to sew piecework for a garment factory. I always watched her from the hallway. Quietly, she would rummage through a purple basket and pluck a needle from her pin cushion. She would unspool the thread, then moisten its tip with her tongue like a cat tasting a warm bowl of milk. I would hold my breath. The thread, stiff and straight, would travel through the air in a decisive line and, without hesitation, pierce the needle's head.

Perfect!

That nightly act of unwavering precision fascinated me. I would return to bed believing in magic. Uncoordinated, with poor eyes (even as a child) and nervous hands, I considered threading a needle—no matter how big its eye—beyond my most stubborn attempts. My mother, however, made it appear like a simple accomplishment, a delicate motion of great consequence. She rarely missed on the first try.

She sewed, my mother did, as though listening to music—with the crescendo of short, fierce jabs or the andante of long, slow strokes. For hours every evening, long after the children had gone to bed, she would stitch pearls onto collars, sequins onto sweaters, buttons onto blouses, and hems on sleeves, slacks, dresses, skirts, shirts, what-have-you. For this she earned a pittance. In those first hard years of exile in Miami, though, it was manna. Anything would have been.

I was young, surely no more than seven, when my mother moon-lighted for a garment factory that delivered its orders and supplies to our duplex every week but was not as predictable, from what I gathered in overheard conversations, about payment. Her day jobs appeared to be steadier. First she began at *la tomatera,* where she and other refugee women sorted tomatoes and picked out bruised fruit. She left for the packing house before we woke for school but was home by the time we returned. Later in life, she worked at a shoe factory, stitching soles to leather uppers. I never saw where she worked, never knew whether another yellow light of an ugly ceramic lamp guided her hands somewhere else or whether the din of machines later echoed in her sleep, an offensive reminder of how a beloved hobby can turn into grating need. She never talked about her job. That was something she did outside the home, when I was at school and busy with my own life, so her silence and my ignorance made her work seem unreal. Real was what I witnessed at home, the nightly routine, the threading, the trimming and the cutting, the glint of the raised needle, the sparkle of a sequin, that orchestrated movement governed by a musical score I could not hear.

By the time Vicki, my middle sister, and I were old enough to help around the house, my mother had stopped sewing for money in the evenings. Instead, after coming home from work at the shoe factory and on the weekends before piano lessons and excursions to the beach, she devoted herself to teaching us to knit, embroider, crochet, cross-stitch, and—during one particularly ambitious period—how to draw a pattern with dart and seam lines. We learned to clean and cook, scrub bathrooms, iron clothes, fold laundry, all those skills she treasured as symbols of her worth and our future. Reluctantly I did what was required. She claims that as a very young girl I performed domestic duties like an unreformed sinner practicing penance: "You watch, Mami," I vowed. "I'm going to make enough money one day so I can *pay* somebody to do this."

I've kept that vow, but my mother still judges me by the house I keep and the meals I serve.

Of course, on occasion I do sew. I hem a skirt or attach a button, nothing elaborate, just survival. Yet, in the mornings when I sit at my desk, a keyboard instead of a sewing machine at my disposal, I thread a narrative through a chapter and embroider the outline of a character. Every synopsis, however simple, is carefully basted. In the final editing stages, I loosen seams, I tighten stitches. I mend. Every day I use what my mother taught me.

To write about one's mother is to court sentimentality. The writing itself is a civilized form of betrayal. One risks everything—privacy, a misunderstanding of complex emotions, the relationship itself—for a recounting that can easily be marred by a banal phrase or a sappy scene. A mother, a good mother, becomes larger than life over time, a source of inspiration, a figure to worship, occasionally a reason for torment, too. As a mother myself, I know that we play a commanding role and create an irrevocable bond in our children's lives, regardless of the qualifications we bring to the part. Through her and with her, we learn to trust, to be intimate, to accept and give of ourselves. A mother's love is yardstick and buoy, haven and catalyst, and so the symptoms of a broken relationship with a mother spread far into the future. What we have—or don't have—with her affects the way we make our friends, how we love our mates, the way we treat our own kids. (Sure, children can and have overcome the fissures of a cracked relationship with this foremost of loves, but that is rare and as difficult as anything we will ever do.)

That is why I write about my mother with such trepidation. Words seem meager, sentences anemic, when trying to describe the various layers, so dense, so rich, of this relationship. Still . . . to write about her is to draw closer, to understand better.

My mother was twenty-four years old when she fled Communist

Cuba alone with three children under six years of age and an anxiety that surely must have gnawed away at her soul. She did not know what awaited her or if she would ever again see her mother or my father, who were fighting in the anti-Communist underground together. In the safety of later years and in a democratic country, I conjure up a young woman walking hand in hand with her children down the corridors of Havana's José Martí Airport and immediately think of a poignant movie scene á la *Casablanca*. My scene would be more somber, of course, with graver consequences: a woman alone, a woman without marketable skills heading for a world she knew nothing about, in a present the past had not prepared her for, with a future she could not trust.

Where did she find the courage to do this? How did she gather the strength to face the uncertainty of a new life? Could I have done the same?

You do what you have to, she says now. In the face of necessity, you can do anything.

You can do anything.

I grew up believing that, never quite realizing it was a tough and tricky lesson to teach in a culture full of constraints, where women learn early on to know their place, where too often their lives are spent compensating for their men. Yet, in many ways, exile was a form of liberation for my mother, as it still is for many Latin-American women who have come to the United States. She was able to do here what she might never have done in her own country. (Necessity forces doors open; if not completely, at least enough to be left ajar.) Here, she learned to drive, she worked outside the home, she developed interests separate from my father's, she lobbied and cajoled and negotiated her way around, usually with us children as her interpreters and occasionally at the mercy of her broken English.

Her English.

Along with her sewing basket and rhythmic needle, one of the earliest memories I have of my mother is of her laboring over a green notebook. On its lined paper, neat handwriting swirled the words of this strange language into a shape that made it more accessible to her. Sentence after sentence had been laboriously copied from a blackboard in an adult education classroom. But as we grew older and my younger siblings arrived, learning English became less urgent or necessary. In the shoe factory where she worked, many spoke Spanish, including the forelady. In the neighborhood, all the English speakers moved out, the predictable white flight, and the new neighbors spoke Spanish. Eventually the adult classes were replaced with children's piano lessons, the green notebook with elementary school textbooks.

In 1997, my novel, *The Chin Kiss King,* was published. On book tour, I was frequently asked if my family had read it and what their reaction had been. I answered honestly: I do not come from a family of fiction readers. Economists, pharmacists, lawyers, and doctors, they read newspapers, journals, and manuals. What's more, I added, my mother's English was so poor that she was waiting for the Spanish translation.

The first people in line to meet me after one program were two gray-haired women ready for battle. Before they opened their mouths, I had already recognized the signs. There is a certain expression we wear—a grimace or a scowl, a disfiguring grin—when we are the first to cast stones. Self-righteousness is such an ugly thing.

How long has your mother been in this country? they demanded. Why hasn't she learned English? Isn't she ashamed to be so ignorant? Does she expect everybody else to learn Spanish for her?

Even as I write this I seethe. At the time, I stuttered some inadequate response. I would have liked to skewer the stupidity of these women, but the words eluded me.

This is what I wish I had said: My mother's story is the story of countless women, immigrant, exile, and otherwise, who put aside their ambitions and their dreams (to speak English, to learn accounting, to become doctors) so their children could do what they could not. The demands of home and factory allowed them little time for self-improvement, and the immigrant culture that could have helped them along sometimes only served to restrain them, simply because of their gender. But their children . . . ah, their children! Measure them by this contribution. In my family, all five of us finished college, three with postgraduate degrees. If education and income are measures of success, our lives say something about my mother, do they not?

"*Cinco edificios he construido,*" my mother replies, when asked what she does for a living. Five buildings she has built, five living monuments.

And yet, her inability to use English correctly mortifies her more than it does us. It speaks to her of a failing, of something that might shame us. When she was dismissed from jury duty because of her pitiful English, she was still flushed with embarrassment by the time she got home. The shame was made worse by the fact that the judge knew me.

"He must have thought," she told me, wincing, "how can such an ignorant woman have such a smart daughter."

This was not an isolated incident. In my mother's mind, situations in which she might embarrass us lurk around every corner and multiply at a daunting rate. It's as though she has educated her children beyond her reach. Best to keep quiet, best to remain on the sidelines. Weeks before flying to New York to attend my youngest sister's graduation from Columbia Law School, our mother worried about making the wrong impression at the event. What would my sister's classmates think? How would her professors react?

"They'll see us and say, '*Miren a esos guajiros.*' " Look at those country bumpkins.

Her reaction is the same when I invite her to events that I think she might enjoy—speaking engagements, award presentations, banquets. What will she talk about? With whom? I don't know how else to reassure her except to insist that being herself is good enough for any occasion. It is so damn disconcerting, her worry, disconcerting to look down at my mother's head after a childhood of looking up at her chin. I am who I am because of my parents. I do not want her suggesting something I do not feel.

Or does she know something I refuse to acknowledge? Does it not bother me to know that my mother has no real idea of how I earn a living? Have I not secretly wished at times to have been raised, as so many other writers I know, in a genteel setting surrounded by books and the discussion of them? Wouldn't it be better if our relationship were based more on common interests and less on gratitude and bloodlines?

My mother was born on the eve of the Spanish Civil War in Sitges, now a posh summer resort but then a small fishing village on Spain's Mediterranean coast. Her mother was beautiful and sweet, with a guileless smile and disorganized ways. Her father was a champion swimmer, a beloved younger son, and a handsome heartstopper well aware of his charms. A notorious flirt, he broke my grandmother's heart several times before he died prematurely of liver disease.

Orphaned, without income after the war destroyed the family's shoe factory and squabbles took what remained, my mother fled to Cuba with her mother and an older sister. She was ten years old. There the family lived a life of physical deprivation. She grew up owning two dresses and wearing her hair in braids. I'm not sure what one had to do with the other, though she always talked about them in the same sentence. As soon as she was old enough, she chopped off her hair, and she has worn it short ever since. I don't ever remember sporting braids, and even in our most dire circumstances, my sisters and I always had more than two dresses each hanging in the closet. We knew such bounty because our mother and grandmother could craft a skirt or a dress, almost anything, from remnants brought home from their jobs at factories. Once my mother helped my grandmother fashion a dress from a curtain. I loved that curtain dress, its burnt orange color and puffed sleeves and covered buttons. The fabric was a little scratchy, especially at the waist and the collar, but I felt so grown up when I wore it, so special. Later, my mother would make my prom dress, my graduation outfit, and the maid of honor's and flower girl's gowns for my first wedding. If I had not insisted on renting my wedding attire, she would have figured out a way to create that, too.

She met my father at fourteen and married him at seventeen. He was twenty-four when they married and ambitious; her family believed him to be quite a catch, this hardworking, smooth-talking college boy. (Her older sister, on the other hand, had married a back-country fellow and moved inland, hardly the upward mobility their mother had hoped for.) Dutifully, my mother began to have children soon after, but that proved to be an inexplicably difficult job. Her first child died at birth, choked by the umbilical cord. In the pregnancy that followed, one of the twins died in the delivery room, and the other, my oldest brother, sustained a mild case of cerebral palsy because of a lack of oxygen. Years later, after she thought the curse had passed, she suffered a miscarriage, then another. In all, five of us would survive. Of her first three children, two were sickly, and I, the only physically healthy one, was, by all accounts, hell in lace-edged bobby socks and patent-leather Mary Janes.

She raised us the old-fashioned way—that is, she was our mother not our friend, she had us follow routine like a sacred rite, and she believed in the adage *Un galletazo a tiempo*. A slap in time. She also knew when to pinch, pull hair, and, when the occasion warranted it, wield the belt. A smart aleck, a back talker, and rebellious, I received more than my share of blows. For the time I slashed my brother's bike tires. For the time I ran away from home. For the time I stole the toy soldiers from a neighbor's window ledge. For the time I smashed my baseball mitt in a birthday cake when the boys wouldn't let me play.

The law was her law, and there was never any doubt about what would happen if you defied it. Domestic democracy was heresy. She did not run a household where children were considered the equal of adults. Nor were they given a choice, until well into adolescence, in what they would eat or wear or watch on television. You did what she told you, and that was that. Every summer, for instance, my mother would sit Vicki and me at the kitchen table to mow off the tresses we had grown during the school year, then apply a perm to what was left of our hair. I hated this ritual, thought it made me look like a boy, and begged to be allowed to wear my hair long. But no amount of pleading could convince my mother, and when I bolted out of the house in angry rebellion, she chased me until she caught me, carried me back to the chair, and tied me there until I was calm enough to be approached with scissors. "This will make your hair grow back strong," she said as she snip-snipped. "And short hair is so much cooler for the summer."

My younger siblings say she has mellowed with time, a slow evolution away from corporal punishment to retribution of another sort. I'm not so sure of that. My younger brother was a college student and over six feet tall when he did something so grievous—I don't even remember what—that she smacked him around. Nor has she let down her guard with the grandchildren. Though she dotes on them, she also keeps a paddle in the kitchen, ready to be used in the unusual case of severe misbehavior. In her house, you may get a second chance, depending on the offense, but never a third or fourth. You make sure you get it right the first time. Regardless of these strictures, my children—and their cousins, too, I suppose—adore her. Her cooking and her rules are cherished legend. The older ones bring their friends over on Saturday nights, and the younger ones plead to spend the day and even to sleep over, which she occasionally lets them do if they're well-behaved. Like other children, they draw comfort from boundaries, from knowing exactly what is expected of them and what happens when they don't meet those expectations.

Throughout my childhood, my mother disciplined in other ways, too. She could be harshly critical and sharply cutting, particularly of her daughters and especially of me. In hindsight, I realize she did not mean to wound, only to correct, but her words often hurt more than the sting of her open palm or the lash of a belt. In her eyes, I never got anything quite right. I was too tall, too thin, too messy, too intense, too big around the hips, too narrow around the shoulders. You're going to wear *that*? Put on some makeup. Stand up straight. Do something with that awful hair. Are you getting enough sleep? If your nose is always in a book, how are you going to meet anybody?

She was still doing this just the other week when, during a family get-together, she decided my dress was unbecoming. She tried adjusting my belt, then fiddled with the collar. Neither change seemed to please her, so she criticized the length, the cut, the fabric's texture. She complained about my hair color: too dark, too strong, too false. Soon enough my father joined this impromptu makeover by observing that my face was pasty and the rings under my eyes looked like a raccoon's. Couldn't I do something with myself?

"You look just fine," my husband assured me later. "There was nothing wrong with the dress, and anyway it's one of your favorites."

I often joke that my parents are a guaranteed antidote in case of a swollen ego, but it's taken time and distance for me to be able to kid about this. I remember looking in the mirror and picking apart all the faults my mother had so cavalierly pointed out. It was a terrible kind of torture, this examination, terribly self-defeating. In high school, then in college and later in life, I found compliments about physical traits—*I wish I were tall like you. You're lucky you're thin. Great cheekbones!*—suspect. The confidence of beauty came very late to me, as it does to many women, and it was not at all the result of parental guidance and encouragement. Then again, it has occurred to me that I have benefited tremendously from my parents' judgmental remarks and opinions. Aging and its consequences worry me little, because I have learned to depend on something more lasting than looks—an unintentional legacy from my mother.

In writing this, I feel a tremendous sense of disloyalty. After all, how do you reconcile the woman who criticized so harshly with the woman who insisted I could do anything, the mother who aimed her husband's belt at my butt with the one who sat up all night at my bedside when I was sick, rubbing my feverish forehead while clucking her tongue? (Her hands were always warm, yielding, solid, and trusting, but also roughened by housework, the nails square and short, occasionally decorated with a dark bruise from some household accident. There was no time—or money—back then for the frivolity of polish.)

Contradictions? Or simply an unspoken understanding that severity had to be leavened with compassion?

A relative once told me that when we were growing up, my mother entertained no interests beyond her children. Her paying jobs were necessary duties, our upbringing her true vocation. This may be an exaggeration, but not by much. She was determined not to fail in the only career she had been given, so she proceeded to devote her time, her hopes, her energy, her *entire life* to us. She employed the zealousness of a missionary. In the name of maternal duty, my mother never relaxed, never slowed down, never knew respite. The first one up and the last to bed, she always busied herself doing something for someone else. Even now she is apologetic when she goes to the beauty parlor, and to see her coifed and groomed—and wearing anything other than her earth-color culottes, Kmart tank tops, and black sneakers—is indeed a rare sight. She almost always smells like she's been cooking something. And she is forever bearing handmade presents to her children's homes—crocheted kitchen towels, knit doilies, lace and gingham curtains. After raising five children, after years of caring for her mother and her mother-in-law through long illnesses, and at a time when most sixty-somethings begin to savor their first moments of freedom from the restrictions of all that is familial, my mother has chosen to take in an elderly aunt and serve as nanny, cook, taxi driver, and homework supervisor for my middle sister's children.

Because of her, I have never hired a babysitter. My friends are jealous and skeptical of this, but I swear it is true. My mother has always cared for my children on weekend evenings. And if she and my father have planned a rare outing on a night I need her to watch the children, she either cancels or cuts it short. When I try to circumvent her offers, embarrassed to pile on more work, embarrassed that my social life should take precedence over hers, she gets angry. "Are you trying to take the children away from me?" she accuses.

Part of the journey of growing up and having children is arriving at a point where you give your own parents the benefit of the doubt. That's where I find myself now. In raising us, my mother did the best she could with what she had and what she knew. Like her, I've learned that mothering is complex and complicated, inspiring and depressing, demanding and entertaining, a thankless task full of contradictions. Someone once called it a vocation of reverse order: you take on the job and learn while doing. I believe we never fully master it.

I have reared my children different from the way my parents raised me—more liberally, less authoritarian-like, with a grip that was not always as firm as it should have been. In hindsight, I wonder if my mother didn't do the better job. There is a hunger in my belly, a commitment and discipline that my children have not displayed yet. The jury's still out on my parenting performance, but hers has strong ratings.

It is only now, so many years after leading separate lives, that my mother and I have managed a friendship based on what she has already accomplished and what I am in the process of completing: raising children. I cannot claim that I am the closest to her of her daughters, though she is the first one I call when something doesn't go as it should. We are not confidantes. Our interests are so vastly different, my schedule so full of other responsibilities. When she needs something, she usually turns to my two younger sisters. They go shopping together, they trade errands, they gossip for hours. Once, when my father complained about the long-distance phone bill my mother had racked up talking to my younger sister in New York, I recognized that twinge of jealousy and remorse. What could they possibly be talking about for so long?

I can claim, though, her respect and admiration. I may not have learned her lessons of domestic duties well, but I have applied the principles—of diligence, perseverance, loyalty, of subtle strength and quiet courage—to areas she probably never would have predicted. In my career, success is measured in awards and rewards, monetary and quantifiable. But the true measure of *her* work is rarely remunerative. It is more about timelessness and continuity, about values passed on and lives lived accordingly. So different, the worlds we have chosen to excel in. Yet, as a sometimes baffled seamstress with the fabric of my own children's lives, I know there is nothing quite as useful as having a time-tested blueprint to imitate, a pattern with which to guide scissors and stitch.

Ritual and Refrain
Scenes of a Miami Summer

And so it is summer again, already, summer with its hot breath and wet lips and whispered promise of release from strictures. On the calendar May parades, only May, but the mercury is rising, rising, a sure sign of summer, and I feel suddenly, almost wantonly, like a young pupil anticipating the recess bell.

What is it about summer—besides its sweltering mornings and rainy afternoons, its beach weekends and ripe mangoes—that calls to our hedonistic yearnings? Seems to me that summer is more than a thawing out. After all, in Miami we can claim but two recognizable seasons: hot and wet, less hot and less wet. Of those, summer beckons like a key to a padlock. Summer translates into freedom from school, from clothes, from responsibilities. Summer is fishing. Summer is surf and sand, cold watermelon, frozen pops, wet towels, thunderstorms and lightning, mosquitoes, outboards, long days and muggy nights, hair tinged green by pool chlorine. Summer is yet one more stab at youth.

For my family, Memorial Day Weekend has marked, as long as I can remember, the start of this annual reprieve. It serves as the official launch, the left parenthesis to three months of slow, heated living. By the time the right parenthesis arrives, Labor Day, we are ready for fall: tanned, relaxed, and eager for routine.

A child of the tropics, I am partial to summers. The first whiff of coconut tanning oil brings back pleasant memories of Sundays at the beach and naps under palm trees, of smoky grills, sweaty children, and backyard fireworks. Summers give me back the evening wrapped in the clear cellophane of Daylight Savings Time. No need to hurry around to dinner after arriving home from work. Sun's still up, and lazing away the dusk becomes the most enjoyable part of the day. In the morning there are no mad rushes to school. No one checks attendance at day camp, and three tardy notices don't earn anybody a detention.

I once thought of myself as the kind of person who would spend one summer backpacking through Europe, the next through Asia, and another through South America. It seemed the perfect way to re-create the freedom of childhood, but I have never backpacked anywhere and maybe never will. No longer want to, either. I've realized that even as I dreamed of the foreign and pretended to dabble in the exotic, I clung to the ritual and refrain of my Miami summers. There is something predictable, and blessed, in them, something comforting. For the long haul, I need the reassuring familiarity of a pattern, of the inevitability of one summer like the other, one season leading to the next. The guarantee of a Sunday anchored on the north rim of Elliott Key, of vacationing relatives who stay too long, of day after day of identical steam and thunder forecasts—these are the kinds of things that help me through those fall and winter months when frantic routine rules all.

Oh, yes, summer is easy. The air conditioning hums tirelessly. Barbecue sauce scents the air. And swimsuits hang wet and shiny on the stiff backs of white resin lawn chairs.

Swimsuit Season

This is the part I hate.

I'm alone in the dressing room with six swimsuits and a very large mirror. I strip, not daring to look at my reflection. I slip one foot in, then the next. Pull, shimmy, pull, shimmy, p-u-u-u-ll, shimmy-shimmy. There.

I face the judge, and wince.

Surely no summer ritual is as depressing as trying on a swimsuit. It sets a tone of cringing misery for the rest of the day. After the fitting-room mirror, a darkened storefront becomes irresistible. I glance furtively at my reflection as I walk by, then suck in my gut, straighten my shoulders. In the bathroom at home I check out the back of my thighs. After dinner I skip the ice cream and choose an apple instead. Unbelievable the power a yard of stretch fabric has to modify an otherwise rational woman's behavior.

I know, I know. Beauty comes from within. Don't be a slave to society's standards. Love yourself. "Fat" is all in your mind. (Actually no, it's all in my thighs.) Yadda, yadda, yadda.

In spite of pep talks and self-esteem buzzwords, this fact remains: Swimsuit fittings are a uniquely harrowing feminine experience. Men, they have few options. Boxer shorts or minuscule Speedos, and I have yet to meet anyone who looks stunning in the latter. The boxer-short style, on the other hand, remains a wise choice regardless, since it's almost impossible to look bad in something that covers so much territory so discreetly. We women should be so lucky.

We are overwhelmed by choices: one-piece or two-piece, bikini, maillot, tank, skirted bottom, boy-cut, or hi-rise. Do all these options help us when we step into the fitting room and stare at the mirror with a critical eye? Ha! It has taken me years of achievement to build up enough self-confidence to accept all my unsightly dents and bulges, and even then, when I pull at the straps of a suit, I still expect to turn into Elle Macpherson on the cover of *Sports Illustrated.*

If the feelings of my friends—middle-aged, middle-class, middling-happy working mothers—typify the emotional waters out there, then beach-related depression has increased as the size of swimsuits has shrunk. Consider the scantiness of current styles and you'll understand. There is only so much you can do with stripes, under-wires, and tummy-control lining.

I'm not ready to turn in the beach towel, though. Not now, not yet. I love the sand and the ocean too much. The misery of pull-shimmy-pull-shimmy-shimmy under fluorescent lights is the price I must pay for such delights. Besides, I still have high hopes for a return to the 1920s knee-to-neck cover look. In the meantime, I'll avoid fitting rooms.

Beach Bums

Hot. Sunny. A cloudless lapis lazuli sky. The beach calls. The children decide to trade the chlorine of the backyard pool for the saltiness of ocean and the sandpaper texture of shore. So we prepare. And prepare. And prepare.

We begin by collecting the important items, beach toys for the younger children. Pails and shovels and sifters and shell molds and rakes and water guns and floaties and beach balls and inflatable wings. Two of each so the younger boys won't fight. Then we hunt for swimsuits, beach sandals, cover-ups, and clean towels. This requires a fair amount of sleuthing because we live in a house where nothing's ever where it should be and shoes divorce their mates as soon as they cross the threshold.

By the time we finish gathering our possessions—including the beach umbrella, sandwiches, chips, a book, three different kinds of tanning lotions, a radio, one cooler with water, and another to store drinks—the children have fought four times. I have threatened them with the umbrella at least once. I think of long-past footloose years, when all I took to the beach was a towel and a friend.

We head east—and promptly get stuck in traffic. We stew in the van. The children fight. The adults get a headache. The air-conditioning gasps.

Finally we arrive and begin the arduous search for a parking space. Miami Beach has many wonderful attributes, but plentiful parking is not among them. So we unload on the sidewalk, dodging in-line skaters, cyclists, two men in drag, three women fighting, a gaggle of camera-toting tourists, and a once-topless sunbather fumbling with her breasts. The other adult drives off in search of a meter, and we breathe deeply the smell of brine and beer.

Ah, the beach!

We spread the towels. We open the umbrella. We distribute the toys. We lather on the lotion.

The towels get sandy. The umbrella blows away. The toys start fights among the boys. The lotion stings open wounds.

But, the water is refreshing and clean. I pretend I'm floating away.

Then the children argue some more. The umbrella blows away again. And the clouds arrive, bruised and swollen with thunder and lightning. The smell of ocean has been replaced with the perfume of incoming rain.

We gather the towels and the umbrella and the toys and the lotions and the coolers and the food and the radio and the floaties and the balls. And the children, of course.

A fat raindrop hits the youngest on the nose.

"Lloviendo!" he squeals. Raining.

Time to flee. We've been at the beach for less time than our investment in the parking meter entitles us to. But, to paraphrase a popular bumper sticker, two hours at the beach is better than a full day at work.

Fast Boat to Paradise

Aim the bow south, through the murky waters of the channel, between the markers topped with dozing pelicans, then out to open sea, and you will head for Paradise. It is a bump-bumpy ride across the crests of white-faced waves, with wind whipping hair and ocean spraying faces, but then so is the road to heaven. You wouldn't really want it any other way. Besides, if you go fast enough and far enough, hand steady on the throttle, nobody and nothing can catch up to you. On a weekend, that is the best feeling in the world. Whoo-pee!

We anchor within view of a shoreline of drooping mangroves and sleeping snook, halfway between heaven and earth. Here, the waters are ribboned green with seaweed, the bottom dotted with sponges the color of caramel candy. Minnows dart. The lapping of the waves and the rare roar of a motor provide the rhythm to the morning's song. Of this I sing.

I come here as often as I can, whenever I can weasel my way onto a boat or anything that floats with any degree of safety. I care little about who captains the vessel, though most of the time I find that I'm heading to this place of peace and solitude with a man—my brother, my brother-in-law, my husband. Boating is a man's thing, and I don't care a feminist iota about the unsinkable truth of this. I just want to get to a place where boundaries are shifting but its inhabitants permanent, where nature's noise is a sweet lullaby sung in the key of patience.

I grab an inner tube and jump overboard. Brrr! I shake the water from my hair, lick my lips. So tasty, salt of the ocean. I hook a line between my small ship and its mother vessel and, with my face shaded by a baseball cap and my body marinating in the sea, I drift. My goal is to think of nothing and therefore to consider everything. I fall asleep.

Around lunchtime we are joined by friends of like mind, land-lubbers by week, water-seekers at its end. They tie their boats to ours, twisted nylon rope stretching from railing to cleat, bow to stern. (The boats lined up in an uneven row remind me of children playing Red Rover during recess, arms entwined, faces to the sun.) Once this maneuver is accomplished, the guys hop from deck to deck to check out each other's equipment and talk shop.

Boating may seem to be a pleasurable way of motoring to the islands and getting away from it all, but this is merely the cover story guys offer their wives. Boating is really about owning the most trappings, the most spacious cabins, and, of course, the biggest engines (Johnson or OMC, Mercury or Yamaha, Volvo or Evinrude). I've known boaters all my life, watched them acquire trinket after trinket, gadget after gadget, an inexhaustible progression of must-have thingamajigs that are as delicate and serious as a teenager in love.

Their vessels are adorned with the latest in navigational devices, festooned with a dizzying array of VHF radios and depth- and fish-finders. To watch the men in my life gab with other captains about the comparative merits of engines (inboard or outboard), tops (Bimini-canvas or fiberglass), and rod racks (stainless steel or Star-board) is to understand that at the heart of all things male there is competition, rivalry, posturing. Funny that it should be evident even in a place where the seamless blue of sea and sky calls for re-pose, a break from the rat race.

"Look at this beauty," a friend bragged to my brother-in-law and two other guys one Sunday afternoon. He gleefully pointed at a super-duper GPS (global positioning system) that can store more way points, or coordinates, than anyone thought imaginable. Wide-eyed, the men were duly appreciative. What six-foot swells could not do, envy did: My brother-in-law turned green.

After examining the GPS, the men hopped over to the next boat to investigate the newly installed air conditioner in a cuddy cabin the size of a walk-in closet. From there they moved over to another vessel where the cabin bathroom included not only a toilet but a fresh-water shower, too. Oohs and aahs punctuated the slap of the foam fenders against the boats. Wives rolled their eyes. I didn't. I swear I didn't. I smiled.

Each of us, I believe, gets to Paradise—our individual version of it, at least—in one manner or another. We need to be certain of our bearings, comfortable with our route, and familiar with the channel that runs from one harbor to another. Devices of any kind are wel-come. Mine happens to be an inflatable inner tube. Bobbing hap-pily in the water, groggy from sleep and emptied of judgment, I remain content to think of nothing and consider everything.

Sand Castles

The city is closed. Everyone seems to have packed up and moved out, on vacation till Labor Day. We remain. From our living-room

window, across the yellowing grass and down the empty neighborhood street, we can see the waves of heat roiling mirage-like from
the black pavement. I call a friend who is toiling alone in an office
across town. "I feel I'm being left out of something," I grumble.
Alone in a cavernous downtown high-rise, she laughs. Then she
tells me about a Woody Allen movie in which a character complains
that he is going crazy, but it is August and all the shrinks have left
town.

After I hang up, I turn off the computer and close the door to my
home office. I'm taking the afternoon off. There is only one place
to be in August; the shrinks are all there. My children cheer when
I mention it.

At the beach again, the heat of the sand scorches the plastic soles
of our shoes. In the sliver of shade near the lifeguard stand, my two
youngest sons and I survey our surroundings and settle on a spot of
sand the waves cannot reach. Here we will build a fortress by the
shore, a mansion of seashell windows and smooth-pebbled turrets:
our last house of this summer season's sands.

There is a method to building a sandcastle, a method we lose to
the madness of adulthood when taking time to pack a red pail and
matching shovel seems like a ridiculous indulgence. I try to re-learn
it every year, and after a few lurching tries, the digging-packing-
burrowing-patting technique returns naturally, like roller-skating or
bike riding. By August I've mastered it.

My sons jab the sand with their shovels and slam it into pails,
thumping each load until it is hard and moist enough. Sand too dry
does not hold; sand too wet crumbles. Moderation is called for.
One runs off to collect fresh seaweed washed ashore by the latest
wave. The gardens of their castles are decorated with seaweed: wild
and woolly plants too large for the layout of their sand city. But size
and perspective have no business here. Neither do rules nor zon-
ing. Sandcastle building is free verse and freehand, a lot like jazz.
When you build it with a partner or two, you jam, man, you jam.

Slap, slap go the shovels.

Shake, shake sound the sieves.

Thump, thump echo the pails.

The boys want to build a family compound, a strip shopping mall, a village, an entire city from gritty seashore. So we work in tandem, perfectly choreographed yet unrehearsed, as we've been doing every summer for as long as they've been walking. We don't talk much except for an occasional word of approval or a request for assistance (*Mom, please get the sand out of my eyes* or *Mom, I need to go to the bathroom*). It's all dig, pack, pat, turn over: a rhythm all its own. Just as a tuning fork causes others around it to do the same when it begins to vibrate, our movements fall into a compatible cadence, the same wavelength. If one stops to shake hair away from eyes, the other two builders do the same. We look up at the gulls together, squint at the slipping sun on the horizon at the same time.

It is in moments like these that I have irrefutable proof (if anyone is to doubt) that a mother communicates with her children in ways beyond the physical, beyond what we can hear or touch or see. There is an emotional force field, an interchange of energy that crackles without words. Can they sense it as I do?

The castle has been built, the moat dug. We march back to the car, in lockstep, swinging our arms in unison, our buckets clanging against each other in concert.

Perfect harmony.

Sisters

When I was six years old and a newly processed refugee child, my family lived in an old, ramshackle house with a screened-in porch that doubled as a playground during the sweltering months of summer. Vicki, my middle sister, was my inseparable companion. We played dolls, jacks, dress-up, house, all those games children make up when costly toys are scarce but imagination overflowing.

One afternoon we had set up store on an old table and, with the few knickknacks my mother owned at that time, were pretending to buy and sell and barter. As the older sister, I was, of course, the shopkeeper, and I rattled the cup of pennies with just the right kind of greedy propriety.

Despite the scarcity of customers, business was nonetheless brisk because Vicki stopped at my makeshift counter to buy assorted dry goods all afternoon. The transactions were quite amicable—until she decided to return a heavy metal ashtray and demand her money back. I refused. We argued. She grabbed the penny cup, I snatched it back. We tussled. Finally, she pretended to concede and stomped off with the ashtray but without her money. I returned to the counter to assume my position of rightful authority.

Midway across the porch, she swung around, aimed, and threw

the ashtray at me. It bonked me hard on the right side of the head. I shrieked. Blood spurted everywhere, over my face, my hands, my clothes. I couldn't see, but I could hear my mother and, behind her, my grandfather saying something to me. After some initial fumbling, my mother managed to stanch the blood flow with a towel. She examined the wound. Hiccuping, I scanned the room until I spotted my sister cowering in a corner, paralyzed by the immensity of what she had done. Aha! As soon as my mother turned around, I lunged for her and got in a few good whacks before the adults separated us. It felt so good. There is a certain vicious vengefulness that children master young; it is brutal, primitive, and effective. Temporarily effective, that is, because for a short time it gives the child the illusion that she's in control.

My cracked head, I soon realized, had thrown the family into a tizzy. My parents had little money and fewer English skills, and going to an emergency room was a nerve-wracking event for the smattering of Cuban exiles in the Miami of 1962. Would anybody at the hospital speak Spanish? How would the doctors be paid? Would I need surgery? Was I going to be brain damaged? How could sisters do this to each other? On and on the adults worried.

I didn't. I was gloating: I could not, would not, get blamed for this. No, siree. I might be blamed for a lot of other things around the house—which I often was, and sometimes for good reason— but this time the fault lay elsewhere: on the little shoulders of Miss Goody Two-Shoes. My middle sister was, and still is, a quiet, gentle being, what Cubans call *un pan con ojos,* a piece of bread with eyes. She never seemed to do anything wrong, and if she did, no one suspected. But now . . . now! How sweet the satisfaction of her punishment.

The hours at Jackson Memorial Hospital blurred one into another, and on the way home, bandaged but relaxed, I began to analyze the situation. It wasn't what I expected. If Vicki was punished, whom would I play with? My older brother refused to do anything with dolls unless he made the rules, rules that were entirely unacceptable, and the neighborhood we lived in at the time was not particularly safe. Even if it had been, I doubt that my mother, who was very strict about our friends, would have allowed me to find a playmate outside the narrow confines of the backyard. As afternoons and weekends loomed endless and boring in my imagination, it occurred to me that Vicki's punishment, no matter how well deserved, was mine, too.

So . . . I pleaded in her favor before the parental tribune. "*Lo hizo sin querer,*" I explained to anyone who would listen. She didn't mean to do it, she didn't mean to do it. I even threw myself across Vicki when my mother came for her with the belt. Though not unusual in a family known for its theatrics, this dramatic move became my first conscious act of self-interest masquerading as noble generosity. It was the first of many and, I think, very typical of the emotional tension that textures the lives of sisters vying and confiding in the same household. I did not know any of this then, of course, probably didn't figure it out for a long time either, but now I'm old enough to recognize the chronic push-pull of a relationship that constantly swings between rivalry and alliance.

Vicki was punished anyway. I forgave her but never forgot. That's because her excellent aim left me with a lasting gift: I must part my hair on the left, against the grain, covering the scar. It favors me.

Think about this: The longest relationship we maintain, be it close or distant, hostile or loving, is the one we keep with our siblings. Parents die when we're adults, spouses appear after childhood, friends come and go. But no other person can claim to know us as long as a brother or sister, and of the two, I dare say that the bond between sisters is usually tighter and more complex—more turbulent, too.

I have known sisters who have not spoken to each other in years, and ones whose relationship has been frayed to such an extent that meetings are tense and conversations stilted. In cases like these, the women seem burdened with a deep sadness and a bitter regret for what could have been. The pain of discord sits heavy on the heart.

And the women who have no sisters? I've heard them lament that missing ingredient from their lives, that special bond, even if they are close to their brothers. No wonder we describe a dear friend with a high honor: "She's like a sister to me."

Sisters can be best friends and rivals, prosecution and defense, counselor and conscience, sometimes simultaneously. Like a kaleidoscope, sisterhood encompasses the many sides and shades of female relationships. And though our relationships can ebb and flow, a result of hectic schedules and myriad responsibilities, I can rely on my sisters in a crisis, regardless of what it is and where I am. They're North Star and safety net. In the midst of job changes and divorces and house moves, this kind of security is precious.

Our family history proves it. My great-great-grandmother was a French noblewoman who fell in love with the wrong man at a hot-springs resort in northern Spain sometime in the last century. Prohibited from ever seeing him again, she instead eloped with my great-great-grandfather, the driver/servant of a duke, and headed south to his place in Barcelona, where she made her home in a room the size of my kitchen. Banished from the family, she never saw her parents again and lived in reduced circumstances the rest of her life. I was named for her, as was my grandmother.

Her only sibling, a younger sister, remained in southern France and secretly continued to stay in touch with Anna despite the family's ban. I wish someone had kept those missives, for I suspect the correspondence between the two sisters, separated by distance and class, could have given us a very personal view of the indomitable strength of sistering. Eventually my great-great-grand-aunt married a wealthy man and led a life of luxury and ease. She continued to write her sister in Barcelona, faithfully sending her money to help with Anna's growing family. Always on the edge of genteel poverty, my great-great-grandmother had five children who survived to adulthood. She named one of them after her beloved sister.

Anna recounted the story of her sister's generosity to her children, then to her grandchildren, and those grandchildren told it to my father's generation, some of whom had moved thousands of miles away to the Americas. It is a wonderful tale, to be sure, one that inspires the soul. Ever the muckraker, though, I can't help but wonder what their relationship might have been had the two women remained in the same city, independently wealthy and lusting after the same kind of life. On equal footing, competition tends to intensify.

It is difficult to let go of childhood hurts, difficult to shrug off old roles that are both comfortable and chafing. I'm reminded of that regularly. Not long ago, when Vicki turned forty, the family gathered for a big dinner at our parents' house. It was the usual boisterous affair, with children playing and fighting, adults shouting over each other, and enough food to feed several tiny countries. Just as the ice-cream cake was being brought out to the table, my mother called for silence to honor my sister at this milestone birthday. She told stories about her kindness (all true) and conscientiousness (ditto), then concluded with something everyone has always known. "Of all my children," she admitted for the first time publicly, "she is the one who consents to all my wishes." Several of us hooted. My mother continued, "I know she will take good care of me."

I turned to my husband and muttered: "And I don't?"

Fact of the matter is, Vicki dotes on my mother and is always in tune to the details of what she needs, what she hopes, what she wants. She lives two blocks from my parents, and my mother watches her children after school. They see each other daily. They talk, they commiserate. I am much more self-absorbed. My mother is usually the one to phone me, and she invariably begins with, "We haven't heard from you in so long." Long being two or three days.

And so, yes, I fight the pangs of sibling jealousy, maybe not as often as in childhood, but every once in a while. Enough to make me feel like a slighted little girl all over again.

I am the oldest of three sisters, older than Vicki by two years and older than Sira by almost seventeen, Sira who is better known in the family as Bebe, or Baby. I have no memory of life without Vicki. Because we moved around, our schoolyard playmates changed, but Vicki and I always had each other to pal around with. And to fight with. We knew exactly how to torture each other to tears. I particularly enjoyed dunking her treasured Barbie, her one and only, in the toilet, preferably after pissing in it. She would counter by playing with our older brother and ignoring me. Sometimes she would chase me around the house until she cornered me. Then she would throw her little arms around my waist and kiss me. I hated that; I hated it especially if someone was around to see it, which was when she always chose to do this. So silly!

Vicki was frail and delicate and mild-mannered. I was tall, strong, and had a mouth on me. Our parents gave us cues about the roles we were expected to play from the very beginning. She was the pretty one, I the smart one. She was the extrovert, I the loner. *Pobrecita* (poor) was the adjective that seemed to precede her name most frequently. An exclamation point invariably followed mine. (Bebe, born so much later, had our parents all to herself, and a freedom from labels.) When I tell newcomers to the family about the blisters of rivalry with Vicki, they shake their heads in disbelief. They see so many similarities and such few differences. "You look like twins," my husband told me when he met Vicki. "Your mannerisms are even the same." I no longer think she is prettier, and if she were, it wouldn't matter. But I also gave up believing I was smarter.

Our view of life, how we approach dilemmas, the way we raise our children—these issues are now, in full swing of adulthood, what truly differentiate us. She is still cautious, obedient, eager to please, as even keeled as a double-hulled yacht docked in a river marina. I remain ambitious, trying, willing to take giant, angry gulps of life—and then spit them out again. She keeps her children under her wing; I push them out of the nest. Even our choices in men contrast: She likes traditional, I want progressive.

Over the years, the bond formed by growing up under the same roof, of sharing the same parents, of enduring and enjoying the same childhood has been a constant even as our relationship has bent and stretched, grown and stalled. I can't think of a more validating gesture than to see my sister roll her eyes at me when a relative makes a characteristically strange comment. I can't think of a more comforting thought than to recognize a sister's outstretched hand in time of need. I have reached out for that hand on several occasions, never doubting it would be there, never formally thanking anyone for it. Sometimes the hand was good enough for a brief touch, sometimes for a lengthy lift. When my first husband died in January 1995, for example, Bebe had just graduated from Duke University and was in the middle of a self-imposed work-and-save leave before law school. Two weeks after the funeral, she moved in with me. When she was accepted at Columbia in New York some months later, she informed the law school that she would defer a year to take care of business—business being the children and me. She would live with us for almost a year and a half, and eighteen months, we soon realized, is both a short period and a long time to renew acquaintances.

The last time my baby sister and I had lived together was almost two decades earlier. I was in high school, and she was still sleeping in a crib. For much of her adolescence I envied Bebe her freedom, her ability to seduce my parents to her way of thinking. Older, more assimilated, and just plain tired, they allowed her to do things and go places I would never have dreamed of asking for. By then I was married and a mother of three. My window of exploration and experimenting had long been closed, though I wasn't but on the easy side of thirty.

When she moved in, she got more than she bargained for: a house full of children who called her Tía Bebe, a schedule of youth-league baseball that defied logic, and more silly rowdiness than a fraternity house. I got something I did not expect, either. She possessed the relentless energy and the judgmental attitude of youth. That is to say, she worked hard but had too many opinions on child rearing, and they didn't always match mine. At one point, when a friend asked me what it was like to live with my baby sister again, I resorted to a metaphor. If we were painters, I said, she would possess the precision of Rembrandt and I the filtered edges of Monet.

When I began dating, she was aghast, and she let me know it. It was too soon, she said. The children couldn't handle it, she added. She griped and carried on. I was insistent on convincing her: What would it matter if I waited two years instead of one? What kind of parent would live life by what her children thought? I was surprised to see her align with my father (of all people) on this issue, while my mother waffled between fearing for my vulnerability and hoping for a new life for me. It was scary enough to start dating again at thirty-eight, after being with the same man for almost twenty years, but the lack of support and understanding made it that much more frightening.

To this day, I don't know how we got through that bump in the road or what, if anything, made her change her views. Maybe she never really did, and instead only learned to accommodate mine. I would like to think that she had so much respect for me that she deferred to my wisdom, hoping for the best and forgetting her misgivings. I also would like to think that she was as forgiving of real and perceived betrayals as I tried to be. In the end, regardless of what she grumbled about, she was my most dependable sitter, the one person the younger boys never minded being left with on a Friday night.

Which leads me to this point: The depth and breadth of sistering is so expansive, so intricate, that emotions can be both conflicting and cooperative. Where there is strife, there may be yearning for peace. Where there is jealousy, there might be help. Where there is silence, there is also probably hope.

My first novel, *The Chin Kiss King*, was inspired by a nephew, Vicki's third child. Victor was born in January 1989, about a week after I had reluctantly moved my family north of Miami, to Palm Beach Gardens, to follow my first husband's career. Driving to my children's new school that afternoon, my hands began to shake on the steering wheel and my heart beat so hard and so fast in my chest that it sounded like my son's football pads in the dryer.

As soon as I got home, I called my husband, Leo, at work, and babbled my intuition. "There's something wrong with Vicki's baby." I didn't know my sister had gone into labor, but I felt, with a sickening certainty in the pit of my stomach, that something was not quite right. He suggested I phone my mother, surely that would put me at ease. Then he added, almost apologetically, "Try not to overreact to the move and all the changes."

When I phoned Miami, my grandmother told me that my mother was at the hospital. Vicki was in labor, a month early.

Few people have heard of Trisomy 18, a condition in which a baby has an extra chromosome 18. We are familiar with Down's syndrome, a trisomy 21, and know that many Down's-syndrome children attend school and later hold down jobs. Those with Trisomy 18 have no such hope, however. Severely handicapped, both mentally and physically, most do not live beyond infancy.

Victor was born with an extra piece of chromosome 18.

I began writing the novel about three generations of Cuban-American women, and how they react to the birth of a handicapped child, in January 1995, two weeks after Leo died and about the time of Victor's miraculous sixth birthday. I finished it within a year. Though the characters are completely fictional and the plot a figment of my imagination, there are certain scenes—ones at the hospital, for instance—that are true to life. *The Chin Kiss King* is a sad story but a happy book, a look at the redeeming power of familial love and how we learn from tragedy. That, like the hospital scenes, is factual.

I am often asked by readers if there was a real-life Victor. When I tell them, they want to know if Vicki has read the book. What does she think of it? She has never said. Silence, for some people, is a close companion to pain.

My nephew died in June 1995. I was halfway through the writing of the book, ready to sign a contract with the publisher. Just days before, I had told my boss that I consoled myself with an illogical thought: I had lost my husband, but I still had my children, all five, all healthy, all growing. Then—Victor's death, a cruel, cruel twist.

All sorrows, at first, run hard and unrelenting. Sometimes the way they manifest themselves differs, but only like the varying shades of a true color. The pain after my husband's death was worn on the skin. Victor's burrowed deep, a suffering that was more empathetic than selfish. I cried for my sister's pain, for the agony she had to endure as she noticed his tiny Reebok hi-tops on the dresser, his striped shirt in the closet, his jean shorts in the wash. I cried because I knew there was nothing I could do for her, nothing anybody could. Grief is a walk alone in the dark.

Yet, writers try to shine their own variations of light into that darkness. They mine their lives and the lives of those they love. They dig and carve, gouge and sand, cut and paste. They steal. It is our way of making sense of an incomprehensible world. For many, it seems as though writers hold nothing sacred, that nothing is impervious to the analysis of our pens. Perhaps. But in that taking for ourselves, in that hunger to examine and diagnose, we also give in return. Or at least I hope so.

That is true of the gifts sisters give each other, too. Sisters' presents are often what we want for ourselves: the angora sweater, the rhinestone earrings, the red-silk lingerie, the leather wallet with a special pocket for school photos. Occasionally a gift results unexpectedly from anger or hurt, like a scar that forces you to part your hair to the right. Some become heirlooms, the kind of intangible keepsake that may cost one sister but help the other. I'm thinking of my great-great-grand-aunt's generosity, but of something else too. I understand, and not without a bit of mortification and shame, that Vicki's personal loss was my career gain. There would have been no book, or at least not that particular book, without her suffering. But maybe the knowledge of that gain somewhat ameliorated the clamor and confusion in her soul, maybe it gave meaning to something that begged reason. Who knows? At this point in our lives I have lost track of whose turn it is to push and who must pull. Best to do both.

Beisbol Dreams

In a rectangular swath of my backyard, protected by rows of yellowing areca palms and tall banana plants, stands a monument venerated by my family: a batting cage with its pitching machine. When it was first put up—poles cemented, netting stretched, stakes hammered—the new plants were only waist high and the cage poked above the wooden fence. It ran the length of our swimming pool and then some, about sixty or seventy feet. From several houses down, you could hear the whirr-thwank of a pitch, as the motor of the blue tripod machine released a ball onto the rubber wheel that, in turn, hurled it across the distance at speeds an operator could control with the turn of a dial. It was quite a production to build the cage, one of those four-hour projects that turn into a weekend event. It involved several visits to the hardware store, a passel of friends, two paid workers, a string of inventive curses, and more money than Leo would ever admit to having spent. The guy we had bought the pitching machine from, a community-college professor leaving Miami for more homogeneous zones, threw in the netting and the poles for free after he witnessed the childlike excitement with which we bought the darn thing—for the asking price, the very same day the notice was posted on the bulletin board at the park. As soon as we bought it, up it went, this sucker's cage, large and looming, a testament to what grown-ups will do to satisfy a childhood desire. As a boy, Leo had always wanted something like this, his very own cage and pitching machine. So he bought it for his sons instead.

His sons—and their friends. For several weeks, neighborhood boys rang our doorbell, each asking, Please, do you mind if I take a peek at your new batting cage? Most came with fathers who followed their sons sheepishly through the house and into the yard to admire the structure that had been erected to America's Pastime. Alone or accompanied, the boys invariably asked to take a few swings, and then of course the *big* boys asked if they could, too. It was hilarious to watch them, the guys who carried briefcases instead of book bags on weekday mornings, guys trying to hit a yellow ball as it whizzed by them. Brows furrowed, they swung up, they swung down, they swung in the middle—usually too late or too soon. On the rare occasion they made contact, they whooped with such delight that their sons looked hard at the grass trampled under their feet. I felt like Kevin Costner in *Field of Dreams*. Build it and they will come, indeed.

To get the approval of our development's association, we assured neighbors that eventually the cage would blend in with the planned jungle-like landscape common to suburbia. And it has, in its own way, just as a shipwreck becomes part of the ocean floor, out of place but still resolutely there. In the years since the machine spit out its first strike, the palms have grown and the banana trees have borne fruit, died, and been replaced by more. At quick glance, the netting looks like a canopy of strange leaves and the tips of the metal poles like smooth gray bark. Sometimes, when I go out to check the bunches of yellowing fruit, I wander into the cage and stand in the middle, between the backstop and the worn-out pitching machine. I think of my older sons when they were boys in helmets and cleats, and pretend they are not what they are now, men-in-waiting with scraggly beards and voices grown deep. I remember the times I fed the balls to the pitching machine, one after another, when their father was alive, then later after he died. I remember how one hard-hit fastball bounced off the backstop and into my face, how another slammed into my open hand, how one pinned me on the foot. I remember all the ridiculous things we did for love and how, over time, they don't seem all that ridiculous anymore. In fact, they acquire a sheen of respectability.

If you were a Cuban kid growing up an exile in the United States in the 1960s, there were some facts you learned quickly, right along with the language. They were part of the cultural propaganda program that included such truths as *American children grow tall because they eat hamburgers* and *American men make better husbands because they wash dishes.* (Both courtesy of my mother.) As for baseball, we knew that the Winchester-toting star of the TV show *The Rifleman,* Chuck Connors, had once played ball in Cuba. He was even rumored to speak Spanish. We also knew that some of the best players in the majors were, you guessed it, *Cuban*: Pascual, Ramos, Cárdenas, Pérez. In school, they might make fun of your accent and your clothes, the car your parents drove, but on the diamond—well, that was a different story.

I once heard a cigar-chomping old man tell a television reporter, on the eve of the Florida Marlins' inaugural season, that the unofficial Cuban religion was baseball, and I shook my head in recognition because, in my household at least, those words rang with special relevancy. Baseball may have been invented on the continent of North America, but surely it has been burnished to perfection in the heat of the Caribbean islands. Little Cuban boys, and the American sons of these Cuban boys, are weaned on the mitt and the bat, fed the slider and the change-up, taught to venerate Luis Tiant and Minnie Minoso, Rafael Palmeiro, Bert Campaneris, and José Canseco, Tony Oliva and Alex Fernández, Cookie Rojas, Livan Hernández, and Camilo Pascual. *Beisbol, beisbol, beisbol.* This is a religion to which you relinquish your heart, your soul, your time, and, yes, your pocketbook, too. In its creed, a pitcher's mound is holy ground, a no-hitter is akin to a Nobel Peace Prize, and a grand slam is a sure sign from God. A true fan, a dyed-in-the-wool, rabid, take-me-out-to-the-ball-game fan, approaches home plate on bended knee and with bowed head. And from the bottom of their cleats to the tip of their caps, the men of my family are true fans.

Family legend has it that when my father was a boy, he listened to baseball games on an old wireless while doing his homework, and he could recite the lineup of his favorite teams without a hitch. More than six decades later, he hasn't outgrown this fervent devotion. When the Marlins played in the 1997 World Series, which they won, my father spent thousands of dollars buying tickets for the home games. "Don't tell your mother," he whispered in my ear, as he gave my two eldest boys some of the bounty. Not more than an hour later, my mother confided that she was allowing my father to believe he was pulling the teal jersey over her eyes. That's the kind of concession a good baseball wife agrees to. (I was also a good baseball wife. I allowed my third son to bear the middle name of Ryan—as in Nolan Ryan—because the former Texas Rangers right-hander had just broken the major-league strike-out record.)

My parents have been married a very long time, so there are few subjects that require further discussion or heated argument. Baseball is the exception. The first time my husband David met my parents, they were watching a televised Marlins game at my house. I warned him there could be fireworks, and sure enough my parents started arguing soon after. David, who doesn't understand Spanish, wanted to know what it was all about.

"Oh, just the game," I said briskly.

"What about the game?" he insisted.

"My mother wants Leyland to bring in a reliever, and my father says he shouldn't."

He was stunned they would take the matter so seriously.

My brothers were taught baseball because it was so prescribed by an unwritten cultural law, the same law that expected little girls to take the obligatory piano lessons whether or not they had any talent or interest. As a child, one of my earliest memories was of a game at Miami Stadium between Habana and Almendares, two

Cuban teams playing with a few transplanted players. Miami Stadium, since renamed Bobby Maduro Stadium for the man who
zealously promoted baseball in Cuba, was a ponderous structure
with hard seats and not much in the way of concessions stands. Its
claim to fame: spring home to the Baltimore Orioles. Later, de-
crepit and neglected, it would house refugees and become a point
of contention between public officials who weren't sure what to do
with it. Still, in 1962, it was a safe and clean place to play baseball,
the only place outside the island we could cheer for the Almendares, because that was the team my father favored.

It took years before I understood the fine points of the game,
years before the cerebral strategy of baseball, the RBIs, ERAs, and
HBPs, made any sense. My initial attraction was its sensuality.

The singular crack of a bat as wood met stitched leather on a
hard line drive. (Later, in youth leagues, it would be the PWING!
of aluminum.)

The taste of flying clay on a head-first slide into home.

The delicious thwunk of the ball as it struck the sweet spot of a
first baseman's glove.

The sharp line where verdant outfield gave way to red infield.

The pungent smell of a freshly oiled glove.

Oh, wonderful sensations!

That is not, however, why I love baseball now. I love the game
because of my sons. I love it because their bodies in play, whether
rounding the bases or swinging the bat or stretching for a line drive,
appear as wondrous miracles. How can they, children of a klutzy
mother, do that?

We have a hall closet full of baseball equipment—mitts, batting
gloves, cleats, jerseys, pants, helmets, caps, hard balls, wiffle balls,
softballs, a catcher's mask, protectors, equipment bags, cups. You
name it, we got it: a collection of positions and hopes and teams.
Nothing in those Rubbermaid containers, however, matches the allure of the very first piece of equipment my son bought with his
own money.

It was beautiful, that catcher's mitt. Well padded, dimpled in all the right places, its leather smelled fresh from the factory. Darned near intoxicating. It hung in a corner of a small sporting-goods shop, a beacon calling to all the little boys who ever dreamed of becoming Johnny Bench. My son wanted it as much as he wanted anything.

"Whaddaya think, Mom?"

What did I think? What did I think? It grabbed my soul—but I also noticed the price tag.

"You already have a glove," I pointed out. "A year old."

A good glove, too, chosen by his father after a meticulous search of stores. When they brought it home, it was lathered with a special oil and bound together around a ball with shoe string. It stunk up the room for an entire weekend. Now he wanted another?

"The one I have is not a catcher's mitt," he groaned.

No, it was not. It was a first baseman's glove, and it so happened that this particular year, the year he was eleven, the shape of the diamond was to be surveyed from behind a grilled mask.

He traced the outline of the mitt, caressed the hand-sewn seams. Oh, what contours! What firmness and fluidity! What exquisite detailing!

He saw himself in full gear behind the plate, the stands full, his friends cheering. A Technicolor dream.

As a sister to brothers and a mother to sons, I knew how guys felt about their baseball gloves. I sympathized; I once pined for a bisque doll with black ringlets and a pink pinafore dress in the same way, with a yearning so intense I could not think of anything else.

"It's not that much money," he insisted. He could not stop touching the supple leather.

"Look," I consoled, leading him away from this alluring gem, "you can get it when you're older. When you have the money."

At home, after dinner, he brought out a wallet from its hiding place, a secret compartment I had long ago discovered but pretended not to know about. Quarters and dollar bills, an occasional five, were scattered on his desk, counted, recounted. Before going to bed he announced how much money he would need to possess that beauty. A hefty sum, but not out of reach. He smiled beatifically, probably expecting me to pitch in the difference. I didn't. I'm an ardent believer in the principle that the longer the road, the sweeter the reward at its end.

He saved his money and bought his dream. He became a good catcher, too, with steely nerves and an arm that could gun a runner down on second base. He liked the position, he said, because he was in on almost every play. He enjoyed the control, the leadership role. And he took care of that glove as one cares for a treasure of immeasurable value. Which it was, what with all those hopes stitched tight along its seams.

Some years later, though, he met quicker catchers, faster runners, better hitters: tougher, more talented competition. He put his glove away. He learned that in baseball, in almost anything, all the effort in the world won't always get you where you want to be. You need luck, perseverance, talent—and even with all those, there's no guarantee of making it to the major leagues. It was a painful lesson to learn, but one that all of us are taught sooner or later, and always the hard way. As his mother, as the witness to his dream, I ached for him, knowing all too well that the recognition of our limitations stings like a hard-thrown ball against a bare hand.

My oldest son was five years old when his father taught him to bat. He had already been fielding and throwing since he could walk. But batting, even off a tee, requires much more coordination. It is one of the most difficult feats in the world of sports. After all, in what other athletic endeavor are you considered successful with a .300 average?

To position him at home plate, Leo moved our son around as if he were a rag doll, aligning his legs parallel in a batter's stance, then pushing down on his shoulders and bouncing him around to loosen him up. Again and again his father repeated the instructions: Feet apart, the width of your shoulders. Knees flexed. Body bent just a bit at the waist. Leo demonstrated with his own stance. Then he showed our little boy how to shift his weight, from his right leg to his left, back then forward. They practiced this several times so that the shifting became a natural movement.

"You gotta plant your lead foot real firm. Like this. See?"

Father and son squared off. They flexed their knees, bent at the waist, shifted from right to left, with the lead foot coming down hard in front.

"You're a ballplayer, little man."

Leo worked long and hard at the batter's stance with his son, actually with the two older children, too. It was not a lesson taught in a day, but one that stretched over a period of years and seasons, one that could be reviewed whenever they crouched over home plate. He was forever offering tips at practice or in between innings. You're hitting late. Or, You're kicking the bucket. Or, Flick your wrists. Or, Keep your eye on the ball. Or, Protect the plate. Or, You're pulling your head. On many days after work, he would drag one of the kids to the backyard and, still in his white shirt and tie, groove to the slow batter's dance. Until it grew dark, father and son would rehearse how to hold the bat and where to have it at the moment the front foot touched down, how to go after the ball and keep your head down when you swung, how to hit through and finish high. They practiced until it was a fluid movement of uninhibited grace, a ballet of bat and body.

In fields and backyards across America, this is a common sight. Baseball is passed from father to son, occasionally from father to daughter, too, a legacy from the Y chromosome to his offspring. Few mothers instill that kind of fanaticism in their children, and I'm not sure this will change any time soon. Fathers are the ones who buy the tickets, who take the kids to games (on a weekday during school, no less), who fight for foul balls and autographs. They are the ones who exhibit the proper fan devotion a child can emulate, the ones who teach an eight-year-old how to read a box score and a scorebook. It is often a wordless transfusion between generations, this passion for the game. Like a silent prayer.

My two youngest sons were toddlers when their father died, so they did not have the benefit or the privilege to be taught by him. Sometimes, in trying to fill shoes that did not fit, I caught myself telling them how to align knuckles and knees as they stepped up to the plate. I learned rules and technique, too, answers to age-old questions like these: Is it legal for a runner to run into a fielder who's fielding a ground ball if the fielder is within the baselines? Under the infield-fly rule, is a batter who pops up automatically out if there's only one out and runners on first and second? What is the difference between a foul ball and a foul tip?

Ultimately, though, it was their older brothers who picked up where their father left off. My second son pitched and threw to the younger ones in the batting cage, shouting instructions and insults: "Bring your arm back! You throw like a girl." My oldest son became the youngest brother's T-ball coach when, desperate for a team that would take a four-year-old, I asked a park commissioner for help. She suggested getting a relative to coach. On the field, it was poignant to watch two bookends of the family in color-coordinated outfits, the four-year-old mimicking the sixteen-year-old, cap, cleats, and all.

In the first bloom of baseball love, there was nothing my littlest ballplayer wouldn't do to impress his older brothers, no ball he wouldn't chase, no base he wouldn't run to. What the little one lacked in coordination, he more than made up for in desire. He slept with his mitt and practiced throwing against a wall for hours. In turn, the young coaches coached as if they were in a World Series.

"*Este si va llegar a las grandes ligas,*" my father announced, the same prediction he has issued too hopefully over all the others. This one for sure will make it to the big leagues. I won't hold my breath, but then again . . .

That's the best part about T-ball, the hope. Prophecy comes easy, and dreams are still being minted. Everyone hits—actually, whacks at the ball—-regardless of skill, and no one ever gets thrown out. Riding the pine, surviving a slump, getting cut, all those things that imply defeat, have yet to detract from the passion and the pomp of the game. Size, shape, even ability, don't matter. When you're on the field, clay under your cleats and glove on your hand, you're a ballplayer, little man, pint-size but strong.

So remember, remember: Keep your knees flexed, body crouched, knuckles aligned. Shift back and forward, weight on the lead leg. Eye on the ball. Open those hips. Open, open. Put your weight behind it. Don't lose it, don't lose it. Pull the trigger now now now. Contact!

"Wait Until You Have Children"

On a Mother's Day in the not-too-distant past, after a breakfast of runny eggs and burnt toast with clots of grape jelly, one of my five children—won't say who, as not to embarrass him—screeched at me in his inimitable way: "I can't wait until you die."

To which I promptly replied: "It'll be sooner than you think." I desperately wanted to add "and you'll be sorry," but I didn't. I'm not sure why. Maybe because it goes without saying.

Was I hurt? Of course. Did I think he meant it? No.

He was fourteen at the time, for heaven's sake, a pimply, gangly, hormone-charged, mood-swinging, misunderstood fourteen, and he was going to make everybody as miserable for his confused existence as he was.

At this point, without offering any excuse for his reprehensible behavior, I must put his outburst in context. He wanted me to die for good reason. I expected him to do something—I can't remember what, but take your pick: clean his room, finish his homework, take out the garbage, join the family at Mass, bathe the dog, whatever. And until he did what he was supposed to do, I would not allow him any contact with friends.

The nerve of me!

To make matters that much more interesting on this day reserved exclusively for my maternal pleasure, the raging teenager who had wished me ill was admonished—"ragged on" as the kids say—by an older sibling who had suddenly appointed herself Behavior Monitor. This is the same child who five years earlier had warned, after I had bailed her out of an embarrassing and dangerous situation, that she had big plans for me.

"I'm going to make your life a living hell," she hissed in her best *Exorcist* voice.

"And what do you think you've been doing these past five months?" I retorted.

Both these children, I must add, were once sweet, sweet babies. They hugged me when they returned from their first day of kindergarten and crayoned Mother's Day cards that read: *You are the bestest Mom in the whole wide world* and *Your still No. #1 Mom!* They loved me, oh how they loved me.

They still do, of course, but it is now a love tarnished by my foibles and their awareness, by my demands and their resistance, by the very nature of the evolving parent-child relationship. While once I could do no wrong from my pedestal, there eventually came a time when little of what I did was right. What's more, no matter how much I did, it was never enough. To parent, I've realized, is to fall short of expectations—mine and theirs—and to be reminded of it constantly.

There are many things nurses and doctors—friends, too—don't mention when, sore from delivery but elated with a new baby, you are wheeled out of the temperature-controlled cocoon of a hospital nursery and into the fluid, chaotic world of real-life parenting. The medical profession provides instruction on feeding, bathing, and myriad health-related questions, but there is not a hint of what is to come when that well-wrapped bundle of joy learns to walk (away) and talk (back) and think (rebelliously). The only foreshadowing I ever got—anybody gets, actually—is the warning: Wait until you have children. I suspected the sleepless nights, the interminable colic bouts, the cost of diapers, the pesky illnesses—even, if I looked far into the future, the dreaded sex talk. But I did not know much more than that.

The pain of labor is blessedly physical. It peaks and ebbs, crests and subsides. It is finite, ameliorated, if you so choose, by a little medicine. In the end, its grand finale produces a slippery, mewing baby. The pain of raising that slippery, mewing baby, on the other hand, is an altogether different kind of suffering. It is bittersweet and long-lasting. After you have a child, joy is tempered with hurt, pride sideswiped by disappointment. In the end, you have . . . actually, there is no end. You are a parent forever and ever and ever, with all the blame and few of the accolades.

That said, I love my children. I love them beyond reason, without explanation. And I have loved them most when I've liked them the least, because that was all I could manage at the time.

There is no greater act of faith than to drop a treasured set of car keys into a teenager's open palm. The fact that it happens daily in the United States, the richest country in history, is a testament to the triumph of hope over experience. (Or is it stupidity over common sense?) Surely there are safer and less-stomach-gnawing ways to test parental trust.

Since the first Model T sputtered off the assembly line, teens have romanced cars with all the passion due a symbol of independence. A set of wheels is more than transportation; it is a door flung open to a world of promise and excitement. We may forget the name of our first-grade teacher, even the feel of the first groped kiss, but I have yet to meet a person who can't remember a first car—whether it belonged to him or to his parents. Children panhandle relatives and save up birthday money for the joy of eventually owning one. Grades suddenly rise for the privilege of driving the family sedan. And chores get done, bedrooms tidied, thank-you cards written, grandparents phoned—all for the allure of having a set of car keys.

Enter danger.

In the past year or so: The sixteen-year-old son of a dear friend crashed a car three weeks after he had been ticketed for speeding. Another seventeen-year-old I know has been slapped with five moving violations in fourteen months. He is something of a legend in my house, for all the wrong reasons. One guy has totaled two cars twice in twenty months. A girl hit a parked car while trying to retrieve her homework flying out the window. Another kid blew through a stoplight and crashed two days after getting his license. And in the newspaper the other day, there was a front-page story about three teenagers who were killed in a drag race at two in the morning.

So you can understand why, when my oldest children first learned to drive, I lived with a permanent lump the size of Rhode Island in my throat. My daughter had so many nicks and bumps in the first car she bought—all of them, she claimed, results of hits by careless drivers in parking lots (yeah, right!)—that a friend in a body shop told her to forget fixing them. Not to be outdone, six weeks after getting his car, while at a red light, my eldest son pressed down on the accelerator instead of the brakes and slammed into the vehicle in front of him.

Granted, my experience may be atypical (I don't think so) and my worries totally unfounded (I doubt it), but there is an abiding perception in the adult world that this teen-car romance verges on fatal attraction. We are well acquainted, too *intimately* acquainted, with the speed demons, the expressway zig-zaggers, the follow-too-closely's, the earthquake music aficionados, the drive-in-the-middle-of-the-road hogs. But years ago, when I was first buying a fancy imported stroller that folded to the size of a wallet, did anybody whisper a cautionary word about my future with souped-up engines and mag wheels? Of course not.

Teenagers and cars—teenagers *in* cars—are the reason for more parental gray hairs than . . . than . . . well, than teenagers in love. I hate to write this, but the nosebleed-high premiums for young drivers' auto insurance are justified. Sure, sure, there are plenty of responsible, conscientious, sedate drivers who also happen to be under twenty. I just can't think of any by name.

This sweeping generalization holds true not only for my children's generation, but for mine, too. Mere months after my parents bought a blue Chevrolet Impala, I totaled the car four blocks from the house. I was eighteen, in my second year of college. The Impala was the first automobile they had ever bought new, and it would be a long time before they drove another car off a dealer's lot. Yet, it wasn't all that long before they allowed me to drive their car again, before they hoped and trusted again.

Like me, they loved beyond reason and without explanation. In the shattered-windshield and dented-fender world of parenthood, they loved when they didn't know what else to do.

The crickets are out. The cacophony of their song wafts in on a nippy evening breeze. Under the eerie spell of this serenade, we settle under the covers, my two youngest sons and I, to travel back, far back, before man, before history, before schoolwork.

Back to the Time of Dinosaurs.

Ensconced with our book in the safest of safe places, we explore the Jurassic period together by the soft light of a night-table lamp. For a half hour every night, sometimes more, the bedroom becomes the perfect staging area for wild imaginings. This is the only place where a three-foot, thumb-sucking, wide-eyed, pouty-mouthed mammal wrestles with the sharp-edged horns and interlocking rows of teeth of humongous reptiles—then turns around to fall asleep.

It is this feeling of safe danger that best explains why each of my kids, regardless of temperament, has been enchanted by these long-extinct reptiles. Their interest has been a predictable milestone in their development. Of course, they move on to other things, eventually becoming mesmerized with subjects and possessions of a more timely era—baseball, sports cars, the opposite sex—but dinosaurs are their first great passion. My children's hunger for everything dinosaur rivals T-Rex's voraciousness. We hunt around the library for dinosaur books, stop at shops that display anything dino, and visit museums that exhibit these giant animals in their styrofoam habitats. We have collected—collecting Barbies, X Men, G.I. Joes, Cabbage Patch dolls, Pogs, baseball cards, and Pokemon is something a parent will be asked to do on a regular basis. Anyway, we have collected dinosaur puppets and plastic replicas, dinosaur puzzles, night-lights, 3-D models, mugs, underwear, pajamas, watches, storybooks, and dioramas. Anything and everything dinosaur. In fact, if dinosaurs still lived, I am sure we would have one—Brachiosaurus or Protoceratops, maybe—as a backyard pet.

When parents say they have learned as much from their children as the children have learned from them, I know precisely what they mean. Because of my children, I now know that a small, meat-eating dinosaur's droppings were a mere three inches long, that the neck of Mamenchisaurus averaged thirty-three feet, and that if you stepped on Seismosaurus's tail, it would take about one and a half minutes before the message finally reached its brain. (By the way, these are useless factoids that make for wonderful dinner party conversation.) Beyond that, my children's engrossing concern with dinosaurs has reminded me of something more important: of the excitement of a new interest, of the joy in an all-consuming passion, of the single-minded pursuit of something strangely fascinating. In the relentless quotidian demands of grown-up life, I tend to forget the significance of these matters.

Another night, and once again the crickets are singing and the dinosaurs are stomping about the bedroom.

"Mom, this book says the dinosaurs all died because a meat pie hit the Earth."

"A meteorite, Ben, a meteorite."

"Yeah, a me-meatrite. Is that true?"

"I don't know, but probably. What do you think, Nicholas?"

"I'm hungry. I think they died because they were hungry."

My son got braces on his top teeth the other day, a hefty set of metal, wires, and rubber bands. On the twenty-seventh hour of their existence, a ball chased him around the yard, curved between two trees, bounced against a car, ricocheted from a wall, soared over the roof, jumped a picket fence, and—WOMP!—smacked him right in the mouth: perfect aim.

"I was just standing there!" he blubbered as we applied ice to his bloody lip.

Of course he was *just standing there.* And of course I know this was a once-in-a-lifetime accident, a freak event that put a particularly careless child with new braces on a collision course with the highly unusual projection of a ball and a geological hiccup of Florida swamp and limestone. I'm very familiar with once-in-a-lifetime experiences. They happen to my children on a regular basis.

But about the braces. This is the third child whose teeth I've tried to straighten, and I suspect that if genes have their way, he won't be my last, either. The cost for such a procedure is astronomical and growing, but I do not begrudge money well spent. I would pay anything for a nice, even smile. Once. But twice? Three times? Every time they leave a retainer on a school cafeteria tray?

In the case of my crooked-tooth children, and in the case of other dentally challenged kids I know, the final cost of braces is not the initial sum the orthodontist quotes the parent. Oh God, no! That's just a down payment. The real expense is the money spent on incidentals: bent wires, mangled head gear, missing separators, lost retainers, or—egad!—stained teeth from two years of sloppy brushing.

My son's "accident" happened right around the time I was reading about the cost of bringing up baby. According to the U.S. Department of Agriculture's annual report, "Expenditures on Children by Families," an average family will spend $350,210 to house, clothe, feed, educate, and care for a child born at the turn of the century. It sounds like a lot of money, but frankly, the figure understates reality. For example, clothing is supposed to cost a parent six hundred dollars a year. Get real! Has the government checked on the price of a pair of sneakers lately? Clothed a teen who grows three inches in a year? What about the kid who continuously wears down his pants at the knees? The child who is always losing his socks?

Another item: Child-care expenses for families with pretax income of $60,600 or more runs $1,800 a year for children under two. Ha! Where are they keeping these babies? In a dungeon? Quality day care can easily run that amount in six months or less.

Then there are the expenses that ambitious parents incur in the hopes of preparing their children for the future: Piano lessons. Baseball leagues. Birthday parties. Dance classes. Teachers' Christmas gifts. SAT prep courses. Once-a-week math tutors. Lost library books. Science project paraphernalia. End-of-season team parties. Prom tickets. School field trips. Educational computer games. Internet hookup.

Did I mention school supplies? My eldest son's graphing calculator cost about one hundred bucks. Less than a month into the school year, it was stolen from his gym bag, even though it had his name written all over it. So I dished out another hundred—and told him his physics grade had to be commensurate with my investment.

I could go on and on. I won't, except to talk briefly about one more expense: photographs. I could wallpaper an airplane hangar with all the "professional" portrait shots of my children I've bought over the years. Of those, the sports portraits are the most interesting. I own dozens of shots of my children in uniform: with their bats, in their basketball briefs, twirling a soccer ball, and in their football pads. They've posed in front of a stadium backdrop. With their team. Next to a tree. In the 5-by-7 size and the 8-by-10, too. I've done key chains, magazine covers, and sports cards detailing height, weight, and stats.

In short, I own a small fortune in Kodak paper. And you know what? Those pictures are worth every penny. When I feel a tinge of nostalgia coming on, I browse through my children's sports careers, this visual chronology that traces their lives on the field—and off. Here's one child at the tender age of five, toothless and shaggy-haired. Here's another thinning out from his baby fat. And here are more shots, so many more, showing the strange haircuts, the traces of acne, the telltale enlarging of an Adam's apple, and—oh, can it be?—the shadow of a moustache. Each image elicits a time in their lives, a time in *my* life, that is long past. Not that I want to go back. There were slumps and hard-fought defeats, obnoxious coaches and overbearing parents, endless practices and even longer games. But there was a lot of fun, too, and cheering and laughter and conscientious adults and concession-stand hot dogs.

Sometimes, in flipping through the photographs, the bad doesn't seem so bad and the good becomes better, sweeter. Sometimes, in the remembering, I think of life's paradoxes, of how many years it took to live through all this and how quickly it all passed.

Birthday Parties
in Heaven

"Can God kill?"

My son's question hovered in the air like a furious black wasp ready to sting. I choked on my orange juice.

"G-g-god?" I sputtered.

He nodded, brown eyes so full of trust that I could feel my heart turning over in my chest.

"Can God kill?" he asked again.

The youngest of my children posed that question two years after his father died. He was three years old at the time, a child of dimpled hands and Power Ranger slippers, a child who seemed, for a while at least, unnaturally interested in variations of one theme: death and dying, loss and love, adults who leave and never come back. Heaven knows how I answered his question, probably with something pedagogically incorrect, but I do remember how the pain flared red hot and furious after weeks of lying dully in the pit of my stomach.

As my baby's virtuosity with the language grew, so did the length and depth of his interrogations.

"You're going to die, Mom?"

"Yes, I will, but not for a long, long time."

"I'm fwee and I'm going to die?" He held up three fingers.

"Yes. Everybody dies."

"Does everybody die of a heart 'tack?"

"No, they die of other things, other sicknesses."

"What does the heart attack?"

"It doesn't attack anything. It's just something we say when the heart stops."

"Who wins?"

Who wins . . . who wins . . . who wins? Those two words will echo forever in my mind.

Death, for adults, is difficult to accept, its finality more absolute than anything we know. Imagine then what it must be like for children, little ones who have yet to distinguish between fantasy and fact, between a talking Scooby-Doo and the neighbor's Great Dane. During the first years of his life, Nicholas's little brain worked hard to make sense of conversations he overheard and events he observed, and I swear that when we spoke, I could see his mental gears moving, pulling, struggling to grasp these complex concepts.

"How old is Dad?" he asked me one night.

"He doesn't have an age now."

"Why?"

"Because when you die, sweetie, you don't have any more birthdays."

"No birthdays? No birthday parties in heaven?" He frowned.

Over time, the questions have stopped, though death, of course, has not. In the three years since those gut-wrenching conversations, a grandmother has died, and so has a great-grandmother. Not to mention assorted fish and one iguana. Death is part of his life, an occurrence that, if not common, is at least accepted; so is the confused, piercing sorrow that follows it.

Leo died in January 1995 of a massive heart attack. He was thirty-seven years old. He left me five children, nineteen years of memories, and a heartache so intense it numbed my fingertips.

Soon after, good friends sent me a card with a handwritten note from 1 Corinthians 10:13: "No trial has come to you but what is human. God is faithful and will not let you be tried beyond your strength, but with the trial he will also provide a way out, so that you may be able to bear it." I stuck it on the refrigerator door with a magnet advertising a neighborhood pizza-delivery joint. For a very long time, I did not believe any of it, not about the humanity of my loss or God's faithfulness or a way out of the trial, but I left the quote where it was in case our friends visited.

I remember little of the first days following Leo's death, except the pain. I walked around with a gaping wound that nobody could see, a gash so deep and so wide that I felt I had been nearly cut in two. Whatever was holding the top to the bottom, the right to the left, seemed a tenuous connection on the verge of tearing. I felt I had no heart left, that it had been shredded and mangled and ripped. In fact, touching the top of my left breast was like touching a gigantic bruise, extremely tender but without the telling black and blue. That came as a surprise to me. I had not known sorrow could be so powerfully physical.

For the first few weeks, I endured on the illusion that he was working late, that he was away on a long business trip. I knew he was dead. My head told me so, but whenever my heart rested on this thought, the torment was more than I could bear. I lied to myself, and that was perfectly fine for a time. Besides, he was so much alive, so *here* for me, that acceptance of anything else seemed ludicrous. I could still hear the timbre of his voice as it filled a room, still taste his lips on mine, still feel his breath as he slept, still smell his menthol gel and aftershave in a house where no one else was old enough to sport a beard. I had all that but not him, and I wasn't ready to let go.

The inexorable march of life eventually helped me to loosen my grip, whether I wanted it to or not. Events, small and large, became pummeling reminders that he wasn't coming back, not from this trip, not ever *ever.*

I cried. Even when I thought I was all cried out, when surely no more tears could possibly be left, I wept again, again, again. I cried at anything and practically anywhere. A song playing plaintively on the radio would set me off, not because it had been his favorite or because its words spoke to me in a special way. Oh, no. I cried because the beauty of a musical phrase, the way the notes rose and fell and soared again, seemed unbearably lyrical to my bruised heart. My sobs would be loud and heaving, punctuated by hiccups, accompanied by a string of sighing, sniveling chords. In public, I tried to be more discreet, only because I had always dreaded the display of feeling unless it was on stage, but there were times when tears seemed unavoidable. They sprang forth suddenly, with a mind all their own. I remember one particular day when, in the waiting room of a doctor's office, an old woman recognized my face from the tiny photograph that runs over my column in the local newspaper. She expressed her condolences; I began to cry quietly, much to her (and my) dismay.

The car became my secret place to weep. For many reasons, I suppose. It is self-enclosed, secure, a haven of sorts. When I drive, I tend to be alone, as absorbed in my wandering thoughts as on the road ahead. And no matter how I tried to control them, my thoughts always wandered to that most painful of corners, like the irrepressible tongue that unconsciously seeks the toothache. I preferred the long stretches of highway where it was harder to attract the attention of another driver at a stoplight, but I really didn't have much control over when the realization of death's totality would make me double over with pain. This, I think, was particularly difficult for my children to understand. I am not a crier. Before their father died, they had seen me shed tears once, maybe twice, and always in some finite way. But in the fog of agony that followed his funeral, the children would plead, "Mom, please don't cry. Please don't cry, Mom. Pleeze!" I didn't know how to stop.

There was rage, too, of course, and disbelief, and shock, and sometimes a silliness that was inexplicable. I played with my children's toys. I sat on the toilet seat with my clothes on. I bought gaudy outfits I never wore, though I hate shopping and couldn't afford it anyway. I stood under the hot shower for hours. I starved, I binged, I watched the Weather Channel. I cried again, sometimes without visible tears or sounds but with an inner ear tuned to a keening emitted in a frequency only I could hear.

In the beginning, there was a uniformity to my days: They were all horrible. Grief, you see, always plays center stage. It arrives with a bang and sticks around with all the ferocity of a pit bull. You cannot see anything, feel anything, want anything but its relentless hold. This happens despite the devotion of relatives and the caring of friends. We were specially blessed with wonderful neighbors who cooked and baked and bought our dinners for two months. Yet, it was this very generosity—the purpose behind it—that cut so deeply to the quick. On the fifth day of this incredible burst of compassion, my middle son, then barely ten, threw his plate across the kitchen and shrieked: "I don't want to eat other people's food. I want to eat what you cook. I want to be a *normal* family." We didn't realize it then—how could we?—that we wouldn't know normal for a long, long time, and by then we would have redefined it anyway.

One horrible, terrible, good-for-nothing day was followed by another, and another, an overwhelming string of them, and my life seemed such an irreparable mess. Burnt toast was enough to send me over the edge. Burnt toast, though, was the least of it. When my trusty, loyal van began acting up, I was certain my world, what remained of it, had caved in.

Water pump, the mechanic guessed when I phoned.

Disaster! I thought. Apocalypse!

I wanted *Leo* to deal with the water pump. Enraged, I pounded on the passenger door that was already scratched and dented, and the sting on my hands seemed to somehow alleviate the misery in my heart.

Driving to the shop, I listed those who surely were more deserving of death: murderers, pedophiles, sadists, old men and women, the latest suicide attempt, all the chronically ill farts lying uselessly in hospital beds. I couldn't understand why *my* husband had died and others continued to live, why that random dial that says TIME'S UP had set itself on him, not José, or Bill, or Tim. It was illogical, senseless, unfair. By the time I arrived at the mechanic's, I had worked myself into such a state that my hands were shaking. My anger smelled more acrid than burning rubber, and life seemed as fractured and out of order as the van's water pump.

Incidents like this, particularly anything involving damaged appliances, leaky roofs, spitting faucets, and all the typical brokenness of a house with a large family, sent me hurling into an abyss of grief. The descent was frightening, and I couldn't see my way out. We probably had some not-so-horrible days, but I can't recall them and surely they were few and far between. The pain was that overwhelming. Friends assured me time would help—time, the greatest of healers, the powerful shaman. But I could not imagine myself *not* hurting. No, no, no! The very idea scared me. If the pain stopped, what would that say of me, of what we had had together? It was unbearable for me to think that, if I lived to the ripe old age all my relatives had, I would spend more years without Leo than with him.

So . . . I slept a lot. In fact, I couldn't wait to go to sleep. Misery or worry may keep most people up at night, but it doesn't do that for me. Grief was a sleeping pill, and sleep was respite, the only place I could escape where I didn't feel like an elephant was sitting on my chest. Yet, one night at half past three I was startled awake by a sound. I bolted upright in bed and strained to figure out what it was. The cat outside? The baby? A bad dream? Only silence answered, interrupted occasionally by the creak of the house settling. My heart quieted; I was safe, the children asleep. I reached over for Leo, for the warmth and security of his body on his side of the bed. But in the dark, my hand met a pile of books, stacks of papers, a heap of magazines: reality. I cringed. Then I traced the outline of my face where it tingled. Wet cheeks. I touched the pillow. Damp sheets. I had been crying in my sleep.

Grief, you cannot escape it. It will hound you until you give in, befriend it. It survives even amidst joy and appears especially poignant in the company of beauty. This was to me a recurring, startling discovery. Regardless of what happened in the depth of darkness, there was always the aggressive splendor of morning, the inevitability of living, of making breakfast for the children, of earning wages, of pretending to think straight. The inevitability of pain. I was always surprised when the new day arrived, and with such fanfare, too: glaring sun, riotous color, chirping birds, frying bacon. The nerve of it, the insult. How could life continue when my own perception of time had stopped?

In the bathroom, bleary-eyed and frightened, I would look in the mirror and scream: Whywhywhywhywhy?!

In widowhood, a person dies in her own way, but if she is lucky, if she is strong, she also experiences a rebirth—with new interests, new hopes, new loves. Grief becomes a method of redefining and reinventing, a conscientious task of finding out who you are alone, separate from the "we" you were part of for so long. That is quite a mission, because we mourn without a road map, in fits and spurts, with passion and fervor, as though we are the only ones who have ever felt this way. We mourn the person, the habit, the hopes dashed, the dreams lost.

Years later and a safe distance away, I am still struck by the sense of abandonment I felt when Leo died. It was like being a little girl forgotten by her parents at a truck stop. Forsaken, deserted, stranded. How could he possibly do this to me? I took his death as an affront to all I had counted on. The hurt seemed inextricably entwined with the anger at being left alone—alone to run the household, alone to raise the children, alone to make ends meet. It didn't matter that I understood death was hardly an event he could plan. What mattered was the crush of desertion, the dissolution of a relationship I was not ready to leave.

Letting go of my marriage was a slow, incremental process, so gradual as to seem imperceptible. I continued to wear my engagement ring and wedding band for months, eventually removing them from my finger to hang them around my neck from a gold chain. Even when I began dating, I kept them this way, an amulet for a new life and a symbol of mourning for a lost love. There was comfort in feeling the indentation of metal on skin and—I realize now—comfort in the protection those rings afforded. But wearing my wedding bands wasn't the only way I dealt with the scouring sense of abandonment, only the most tangible.

I cannot single out one act, or even a fleeting thought, to mark the beginning of the letting go. It was a cumulative, repetitious procedure. It took me several visits to the grocery store before I stopped reaching for all the goodies he enjoyed—the Triscuits, the Heavenly Hash ice cream, the crusty Cuban bread—and even when I stopped, my heart refused to give in. I continued to peruse those aisles, those particular shelves, if only to comfort myself with what I had once done. But it wasn't just at the grocery store where the interruption of habit felt like I was being split open. Right after my agent informed me of the sale of my first novel, I automatically dialed Leo's number at work, raring to tell him the news. Someone else answered. Stunned, I threw the phone down. For a moment there, it seemed as if he had never left.

In bed at night, there was such a desolate space where he had once slept, an emptiness that reached beyond the boundaries of the sheets. I tried sleeping on his side for a few days, claiming new territory and hungry for any contact, however imaginary it might be. But uncomfortable with that angle, I returned to my corner and filled his with books and papers, pillows, magazines. The bed then seemed less . . . less daunting. I realized that having the covers all to myself was not all it was cracked up to be.

If there was any clear, visible marker on the way to a dissolution of my marriage, surely it came in the eighth or ninth month after Leo's death, when I began to clean out his closet. I had tried it once before but had collapsed on the floor, sobbing into one of his T-shirts. This time, though, I felt stronger, enough to be allowed to reminisce. Standing in the middle of his walk-in closet, it seemed every item I stuck in a bag—every pair of slacks or shirt removed from its hanger, every shoe paired with its mate—carried a wisp of our life, and our dreams, together: a Hawaiian shirt for vacation, a serious red tie for a job interview, swim trunks for beach outings, Florsheim shoes grabbed on clearance sales, Italian pinstripes for a First Communion and a family wedding, assorted sizes of belts for all the triumphant diets and the embarrassing weight gains. I could trace our history from skinny ties to double-breasted suits. I grabbed his favorite jacket, a well-worn windbreaker he often used for the cool days at the beginning of baseball season, and held it to my face. On the ribbed collar, there were still traces of his Paco Rabanne cologne. When the tears finally came, they did not break with the anguished rush of a waterfall but with the more sedate flow of a brook; I had resigned myself to a life I had not planned for.

As I was getting used to the loss, I was also grappling with the fact that I was single. *Unwed.* It was lonely and liberating and . . . different. Our relationship had been like that of so many husbands and wives, fraught with perils, subject to whims, buffeted by temptations. It also had been—by far, hands down, no competition—the most delicate and labor-intensive relationship I have ever been in. Sometimes we had complemented, sometimes we had clashed. Sometimes I liked what we did for each other; sometimes I hated what we did to each other. Sometimes I shrieked that there wouldn't be any more sometimes. But in the end, our marriage, any marriage, wasn't really about sometimes. It turned out to be about love that sustains between the good sometimes and the bad sometimes. It was about forever. Till death do us part.

And now that death had parted us, I wasn't quite sure how to go about my way.

Leo liked his shirt collars starched and button-down. He preferred blue socks, calf high and never nylon. And once, when I bought him colored underwear, he said, "I'd only wear these for you." He did; I laughed. Leo was a touchy-feely kind of guy, all bark and no bite. He was the quick fuse; I was his circuit breaker. He was in-your-face intense; I mastered the retreat. Yin and Yang, a friend called us. We were not the ideal couple and had far from the perfect marriage, but every year we remained together was a victory for two people headstrong and willful and bent on following their dreams. And we had so many dreams, so many, so many! A bigger house, a little place on the water, early retirement for him, a second career for me, travel, Ivy League education for all the children. It is the ordinariness of these dreams that still clutches at my heart. They could be anybody's, but they were ours, and we thought they would be there tomorrow and surely every day after. Not once did I doubt we would be together to accomplish them, and I'm sure he never considered otherwise, either. I still have dreams, many of the same ones actually, but the certainty of having tomorrow I have yet to recover.

Leo and I met right out of high school. He was editor of the community-college newspaper, I a wannabe reporter. We had grown up five blocks from each other and knew some of the same people but had never been in the same room together. He claimed it was love at first sight. I, quite honestly, thought he was a little annoying. So pushy! Obviously pushy grew on me. We got engaged at nineteen, before I left Miami to finish my education in Tampa. When we married, he worked two full-time jobs to save a tidy nest egg. We bought a condo, and the children began arriving soon after. For most of our early marriage, we worked—as they say in Spanish—*como unos mulos*. Like mules. He got his master's degree, I wrote two nonfiction books—while caring for the kids and maintaining full-time employment. We moved up, away into the suburbs. There were more children. And fights, of course. Over money—he was wasteful, I frugal. Over the children—he was the good cop, I the enforcer. Over the housework—he tried to help, I thought it wasn't enough.

Our arguments, now that I think of it, were often petty. I used to get mad at him for the stupidest things. For leaving dirty socks on the bathroom floor. Or eating the last of a pie. Or reading the newspaper while I was swamped with morning chores. Trivial, trivial. But back then, they seemed so important, so necessary. I was intent on running a household, and that daily effort tended to overpower almost everything. Shortly after Leo died, I remember calling a friend during an evening rainstorm that howled and pounded just like a hurricane. "I'm going crazy," I confessed. "All I keep thinking is that he's out there getting wet."

She assured me he was safely buried, that he was not getting soaked, and then, good friend that she is, kindly pointed out that had he been alive, I would have probably chewed him out for not taking a raincoat. We agreed that the longer we lived with our perfectly capable men, the more we felt that having a husband wasn't too different from caring for a child: You mothered him, you pampered him, you worried about him.

After spending half a lifetime with the same man, I realized I had discovered more about him than belt size and shoe width. I also had mastered how he prayed to God and what he really thought about his boss, what he would never tell his mother, and why he refused to look down over the Grand Canyon after the family had driven thousands of miles to do precisely that. Yet, it was only after his death that I admonished myself for not having learned more—about him, about myself, about the two of us together. That's when I also realized how, if given a second chance, I might have done a few things different.

I wish I had compromised more.

I wish I had complained less.

I wish we had spent more time together.

I wish being right had never mattered.

I wish I had been gentler instead of stronger.

I wish I had apologized instead of sulked.

I wish I had granted more pardons.

And I wish I had laughed louder and longer and when it was least expected.

Too late now. When a person dies, someone you have loved and hated, caressed and injured, sometimes simultaneously, sometimes without knowing—when that happens, all opportunity is gone for forgiveness, for amends, for a final, redeeming word. It is these regrets that leave such a bitter taste long after the pain has quieted.

Regret is something I know plenty about. On the afternoon Leo died, he wanted me to accompany him to a drugstore to buy cold medicine. He complained he couldn't breathe. I told him to wait, the children were scheduled to be brought home from the movies by another mother and I could not leave the house empty. My last words to him as he left alone for the store where he died were these: "Stop being a big baby."

The rack of blue and gray and charcoal extends across the long room to the wall. I look at the size labels and realize I'm out of my league. For this, I think, my legs weakening, my heart thumping, you need a father.

My oldest son and I are shopping for a suit. I know his vital statistics, as a mother is wont to do: size 32 pants, size 15 shirt, size 10½ shoes. I am not prepared, however, for what I see. The smallest suit size is 38. Thirty-eight what? Waist? Chest? Neck? Shoulder to arm?

The last time I bought him a suit—the same blue-gray suit his younger brothers will inherit one after another—he wore a boy's size 10. Life was simple then.

I spot a man, a fatherly type, browsing through the rack up ahead. I suggest asking him for help, or, at the very least, finding a clerk—anyone—in this discount retailer.

"No!" hisses my son. "I'll just try them on."

So he does, one by one, until he settles for a navy blue of polyester and worsted wool.

"Thirty-nine-S," I note aloud, and enter it into my mental computer for future reference.

On to the tie. He wants one like the ones his father favored. I know the type immediately: Looney Tunes. And then I brace myself for the constriction in my throat, the heat of tears in my eyes, the pounding in my head. I've learned that it is events like this, the children's milestones—the purchase of a suit, the preschool graduation, the first date, and the first shave—that are guaranteed catalysts of a pain that still cuts to my heart, straight and unforgiving.

My children don't have a father. This remains the harshest of all losses.

Not too long ago, I watched a friend in-line skate with his son. I watched the ease with which the two talked, reached across to balance each other, laughed at something ahead in their path. I was insanely jealous for my own children, for something they can never have again. I always get that same kicked-in-the-gut feeling when I watch other fathers with their children, ambling to and from baseball fields after practice, pushing swings in playgrounds, sharing intimacies in coffee shops, trading tips at dinner, holding hands at theme parks. I resent it so. My children have been robbed, and there's no court, no judge, no justice to reclaim the goods. They know it, too.

Years after Leo died, one of the boys broke down in an uncharacteristic show of emotion that left us crying in each other's arms. This is a boy who shaved for the first time without his father to teach him how to negotiate the curve between cheek and chin, a boy who still secretly hopes against all logic for something that will never happen. "I keep thinking," he sobbed, "that Dad's going to come back."

There are other men in his life—generous and compassionate uncles, a doting grandfather, a stepfather sent by heaven—but that unvoiced yearning is for a man who will recognize himself in the turn of his son's face, the shape of his body, the grace of his limbs.

Father hunger. Ask divorced women about this yearning. Ask single mothers. Widowed mothers. Abandoned children. Father hunger is palpable in the questions that children ask, the prayers they recite, the way they act in school. It is the corollary, the follow-up, to: Where do I come from? Who do I look like?

It is amazing what very young children remember about their fathers who are gone, and what they invent to be able to cling to something if memory refuses to cooperate. My youngest was a toddler when he spotted his father's broken eyeglasses, the ones he never got around to fixing, and shouted out with glee: "Papa! Papa!" How did he know? What else can he remember?

This father hunger is in no way limited to sons. My daughter has spent a good portion of the last five years in search of that which is as elusive for her as for her brothers. Her father's death followed one of her particularly rebellious years, so she grieved, as I did, with a heightened sense of regret. For months, she had a recurring nightmare where a piece of her father's heart broke away every time she did something wrong. "It seems," she wrote, "that all I have done was wrong, and it took his whole heart, and that caused his death." That sentiment hasn't changed, only evolved. On pink stationery with a teddy bear sitting in a white wicker chair, she wrote on another occasion: "There's not one day that I don't think of Dad. It's such a horrible tragedy . . . I don't know what God has planned for me in the future. I don't know why He lets these things happen. My only guess is to make us stronger as a family and believe me it has worked in my life." Our mother-daughter relationship has waxed and waned, struggled, settled for something neither of us is happy with, yet her rapport with her father endures into the afterlife, strong, nostalgic, unblemished by the reality of daily friction. He has become Saint Dad.

It's tough competing with that ideal. Actually, it's impossible. I'm human, faulty, beset by worries and saddled with responsibilities. While Saint Dad smiles beatifically from his photo frame, I am the one who tells the kids to turn off the Nintendo, who demands homework, who orders room-cleanings, who metes out punishment. I am the one who has been insulted, mistreated, turned away from. I am the one who loses her temper and grows weary from the relentlessness of children's demands.

I'm the one who's still alive.

I think it was Eleanor Roosevelt who said, "You must do the thing which you think you cannot do." I have. I've gone on with my life, jump-started a career, fallen madly, desperately in love. I won't say, however, that I have healed. Healing implies a cure, and I don't know of any for grief. Yes, time eases the pain from a sharp throbbing to a surprise pang and eventually to a dullness secreted in the alcove of the heart. But it doesn't ever take it away. Just the other day while rifling through an old file cabinet, I discovered a legal pad with Leo's scribbles. It was a list of improvements we had planned for our house. I gasped and held my breath. I ran my fingers along the loopy handwriting, clutched the pad to my breast. Oh God, oh God, oh God! The hurt was not for what once was but for what could have been.

For my younger children, his absence has become a presence, like a phantom limb. They have lived more years without their father than with him, yet he remains a central figure in their lives by the very fact that he's not here. They ask questions, not about death and dying anymore, but of what he liked to do, what he preferred to eat, how he dressed and walked and spoke. Even Nicholas now understands that there are no birthday parties in heaven, at least not any like the kind he knows, but he remains eternally fascinated by someone he can't recall. Every night after prayers, he and older brother Ben, lying not too quietly in their bunk beds, finish their routine this way: "I love you, Baby Jesus. I love you, Dad." Then they take turns telling their father about the events of their day: the two-run homer, the new boy in class, the science project that didn't work, a neighbor's pick-up basketball game. These are the same boys who climb all over their stepfather's lap, wait for him at the door when he returns home from work, follow him around the house on a Saturday morning as he ticks off a To-Do list, and beg him to start a new chapter in whatever book he is reading to them. How happy they seem, how perfectly comfortable with the dichotomy of their lives!

Leo took things I'll never recover: a sense of invincibility, the comfort of security, that silly charm of youth, even a certain naivete we had managed to preserve in the midst of our daily travails. At the same time, the aftermath of his death left me with other valuables. If it's true that we learn more about ourselves through our winters than our springs, then the lessons from this Siberian freeze, so icy and bitter and long, could fill many pages of my biography.

I learned, over time, about the faithfulness of God, the solace He provides if we surrender to those things we do not understand and that we cannot control. I learned, too, that survival arrives a day at a time, never all at once. Somehow, hour by hour, event to event, I lived through something I had considered unlivable. Eventually, those days became weeks, weeks turned into months, months into seasons, seasons into years. In the beginning, when I had first received the quote from Corinthians, I had been looking for a white limousine; my Lord gave me a wooden cane instead.

Along with the cane, I also got a new pair of glasses graduated to a different perspective. The eyewear came with important instructions. *In the case of despair,* the insert noted, *always try on these phrases for size: In the grand scheme of things . . . When all is said and done . . . If I were to die tomorrow . . .* I often remember what Leo used to tell me when I was frothing at the mouth over one ridiculous thing or another. "It isn't a problem if you can solve it with money." True, how true. All the money in the world won't bring him back, but a little money, even in the form of a loan, can resolve the pesky problems that sometimes aggravate me needlessly. That's not to say that grief suddenly made me wiser and all my other relationships whole. Of course not. It didn't even inoculate me against other hurts. Keeping a healthy perspective requires constant adjustment, and I use my husband's death as the yardstick to measure all hardships. It is both reference point and dividing line in my life, the ground zero of a personal battle. If anything, that kind of outlook may be Leo's last, and certainly most unexpected, gift to me.

Grief is a lifelong journey, with a defined beginning but no destination or foreseeable finish line. At first, you crawl, and once upright, you stumble through the twists and turns of a path too dark to ever be familiar. It is arduous beyond words. Then one day when you least expect it, you notice that your footing is firmer, your stride longer. You discover markers along the way: damp hugs after showers, the beach before a thunderstorm, the silent music of prayer, cupcakes baking in the oven, the scent of a gardenia's first bloom. And you learn that all you can hope for is not another road, simply a less slippery slope.

Cellulite, Schmellulite

Some people swear they love to work out, just *lo-o-ove* to strain and struggle against the forces of nature and the laws of gravity. They're lying. There's only one good thing about working out.

Having finished.

Okay, okay, I may be exaggerating—but only by a five-pound barbell.

I know what I'm talking about. Three times a week, sometimes five if I'm good, I greet day's first light on some ridiculous contraption that makes me pant and pray that a biomedical company will invent a magic pill to give me the body I deserve. I should be concerned with strength and stamina, cardiopulmonary health and all that stuff, but that's just a bunch of gobbledygook to me. That is not why I exercise.

I work out at the gym because of my thighs. I work out because of my cellulite. There, I said it. Cellulite, cellulite, cellulite.

I am an expert on cellulite. I am obsessed by it. If I win the Florida Lottery, I want to allocate two or three million to set up a foundation to study fat. Not just any fat, but cellulite.

I've tried everything short of plastic surgery to rid myself of cottage-cheese skin. I drink water. Eat albacore tuna fish. Stay away from fat (kind of, sort of, sometimes). I invested in a special soap, then an imported cream, and I've massaged the back of my thighs with a plastic roller. I even considered a new cellulite-reduction program at the dermatologist's, but the cost—and the time commitment—was more than I wanted to pay.

So now I go to the gym.

There, from the mirror on the wall, the cellulite winks and grins at me, teasing and defiant. It is not going anywhere. In fact, I suspect that a year or two ago it began a slow migration south from the upper regions to the no-man's-territory of mid-thigh. On bad days, I envision its relentless march down the geography of my legs, stopping only when it arrives triumphantly at body's end: the meaty tips of my big toes. I know how ridiculous and shallow this sounds. I don't care. If I resign myself to its homesteading on my thighs, I might as well give up on swimsuits and shorts—the most basic apparel for Miami's clime.

I once shared these concerns with a loosely organized sorority of women who kvetch about sagging breasts, droopy butts, expanding tummies, and varicose veins. They sympathized, they commiserated. They recounted their own tales of woe. Eventually, though, they chided me for being preoccupied with the wrong thing. Most claimed that a thin person (me) who wears the same size she did in high school (usually) cannot possibly suffer from dimpled skin. So come back, they told me, when you have a more believable body-image problem. Obviously, they know nothing, *nada,* of cellulite. Cellulite is an equal-opportunity condition, and stubborn beyond reproach. If ever isolated and marketed, its adhesive quality would give Super Glue a run for its money.

Eventually my cellulite whining reached such an annoying decibel level that my exasperated husband ended up buying me a membership to his gym and hiring a trainer he had used. I worked with Mr. Trainer for more than four months. Throughout the program, Mr. Trainer insisted on telling me about muscles I never knew existed and how each repetition strengthened them. Biceps, triceps, deltoids, quads, gluteus, hamstring, calves. Recited in a certain order, they sounded to me like the books of the Bible. Mr. Trainer was not at all amused by my wit, though. His heretical reply: "Keep your scapula retracted." (The scapula, by the way, is your shoulder blade.) Another time, he confided that his secret desire was to open his own gym. I suggested he call it The Inquisition. He barked: "Keep your scapula retracted." That was his favorite phrase during the months he trained me; it echoed like a personal mantra over every pound I pushed and pulled. *Keep your scapula retracted. Keep your scapula retracted.* I bet he yelped it at the doctor when he was born, as soon as he confronted all those middle-age paunches in the delivery room.

Sure, Mr. Trainer was merciless, but he was being paid quite handsomely to be. He didn't care about my personal life, if a child had gotten up twenty-three times the night before or if I was worried about changes, transfers, and cutbacks in the office. I was going to do two sets of twelve regardless. Under his tutelage, I learned plenty about weights and resistance and cardio and, of course, machines, too: Cybex, Magnum, Hammer Strength, and Nautilus. If you have never been to a gym, I recommend you tour one. The first visit is usually free, and you'll be amazed at the display of modern engineering and perverse imagination. In workout parlance, the torture appliances you will see are known by such innocuous names as Leg Extension, Leg Curl, Hip Adductor, Butt Blaster, Seated Row, Fly, Chest Press, Shoulder Press, and so on. Each machine has a little drawing of a human body with a certain muscle group inked in color, usually red. This tells you what muscle group you are working. (Gee! as if burning pain in the area left any doubt.) I once told Mr. Trainer the darn things should be renamed, the better by which to remember them: The Proctologist, The Perky Breast, The Bear in the Woods, The Labor Machine, The Hit and Run.

"Keep your scapula retracted," he ordered, as if he hadn't heard me.

Before he became a trainer of humans, Mr. Trainer trained dogs. When my muscles quivered and my throat released irrepressible shrieks, I wondered if he wished he had stayed in that line of work. There were times—especially when he told me there were only three more, two more, come on, come on, one more, you can do it—I thought of biting him. I didn't because I feared he would order another set at the angled leg press.

When he moved on to two-legged creatures, Mr. Trainer began judging body-building contests where men showed off biceps the size of my waist. I think I provided him with a change of pace, a comical outlet, like a Jim Carrey movie after a steady diet of Meryl Streep. With me, a weakling of little exercise experience and even less coordination, he was patient but unbending. He was encouraging, too, cheering a variety of victories, including the first time I lifted eight-pound dumbbells with considerable ease. Still, I had my doubts about his allegiance. I wondered if later, remembering my session, he doubled over with laughter in the privacy of the gym's bathroom stall.

Despite our love-hate relationship, we still managed some fascinating exchanges, the kind you share with your dentist when he's filling a cavity in your left bottom molar. Our conversations sounded like this:

MR. TRAINER: How does it feel?
ME: Grunt.
MR. TRAINER: Can you squeeze out another one?
ME: Grunt!
MR. TRAINER: Looking pretty, looking pretty.
ME: Grunt! Grunt!

Though he has not trained me now for a very long time, we still run into each other at the gym, teacher and student, and our relationship has not budged an inch. He is forever correcting my posture, my weights, my attitude. But I do keep my scapula retracted.

For about thirty-five years, I was one of those people who believed exercise consisted of watching ESPN's *Body by Jake* in the mornings after a light breakfast. If I wanted a more strenuous workout, I hauled out the baby stroller to push the baby while following an older brother on his tricycle around the block. The pace varied anywhere from a lazy amble to a gentle trot. I had not the least desire to prance around in Lycra leggings.

Oh, I had tried to exercise, but only occasionally and without too much commitment. For a while, I rode a stationary bike in the garage, which was okay if you like that type of thing, going 'round and 'round and 'round without the landscape changing. But after a month of that, with only garden tools and recycling bins for scenery, I pinched my thighs, found them as soft as cookie dough, and shrugged in surrender. Another year, I began jumping and flailing to the beat of an exercise video while my children ate breakfast. When a business trip took me to five different cities in twelve days, though, I felt foolish hopping around my hotel room. Back home again, I couldn't find the video. Later I also took up—and gave up—jogging, tennis, and swimming.

A year shy of the big Four-O, I began to walk in the very early morning, when night had yet to cede to the day's routine. Walking—walking fast against the wind, pumping arms, breathing hard—was perfect at that hour. I stuck to it for a long time, longer than with any other form of exercise. I think it was because it offered me a half hour of silence, a seldom observed celebration in my life, and because it required no fancy equipment, just an old T-shirt, shorts (sweats on the rare days the mercury dropped), and a good pair of sneakers. I walked the same route at the same time most every day, refusing to venture into uncharted territory. I came to know the dips and twists, cracks and crevices of the two-mile stretch. I enjoyed it. On my course, a blooming tree—jasmine? henna?—perfumed the air. Dew draped leaves, grass, twigs, branches. Birds rustled in nests. And toward the end of my walk, as I turned the bend back to my neighborhood, light seeped into the line of horizon and soaked the scalloped edges of new clouds. It was a pure and perfect pleasure.

The texture of my thighs, however, remained the same. That's when David suggested his gym. Before working out with Mr. Trainer, I had been in a gym once or twice, in my early teens, when I accompanied my mother to one that had opened as a storefront. Gyms were different back then, as were the machines and society's attitude toward physical fitness. This was before aerobics and spinning and Tae-Bo and step exercises and personal trainers. Way before. For instance, my mother's routine consisted of strapping herself onto a vibrating belt that massaged her hips and thighs in such a way that if she tried to talk she sounded all quivery, like a bad voice-over of Mickey Mouse. I guess the idea was to dissolve those fat molecules by sheer force. It didn't work.

You know that old adage, No pain, no gain? It's true, sadly. And my generation knows it. We have, more than any other group before us, elevated working out to a religion. Yes, it is a religion followed by very few—the number of overweight, unfit people seems to be on the rise—but they are a fanatical few, zealous enough to capture the curiosity and envious admiration of the masses. I need only point to the proliferation of exercise videos, sporting-goods stores, and personal trainers to prove that almost everybody, at some point in their lives, has tried to get in shape. We all have some measure of vanity; we differ only in how much we'll do to satisfy it. Exercising speaks eloquently to that silent narcissism. Oh, sure, a workout routine or a two-mile morning jog is good for health and physical well-being, but its unvoiced promise is also about something more tangible: a trim, youthful look.

As a result of this exercise frenzy, our concept of beauty has changed gradually. It is not enough to be thin; one must be fit, too. A woman with just the right kind of muscle definition—the kind of body shape that my grandfathers might have looked askance at—is now sexy and desirable. We do not want to be Rubenesque models, but we don't want the waif-like Twiggy, either. We want to be Sandra Bullock benching a hundred. (Well, maybe sixty.)

I work out at a serious gym. Men and women go there primarily to build muscle. Nonetheless, the gym has a culture all its own. Mine is decorated in black and aqua. The bulletin board advertises body-building contests, health bars, houses for sale, and wisdom like this, from *The National Enquirer*: "Inflation marches on, making it possible for people in all walks of life to live in more expensive neighborhoods—without ever moving." A few feet away, a blender and a coffeemaker sit in the nook of a wet bar. Here designer protein shakes—Myoplex, Apex, Hero Tech—are sold for four bucks. A cutout of Mike Myers as Austin Powers is taped to the white refrigerator door. One of the staff members has bubbled this quote over the character: *I put the PRO in protein shakes, baby.*

The gym provides several classes in the mornings and late afternoons: spinning, aerobics, Jazzercise, body sculpting, yoga. It's mostly women who take these, though an occasional man will brave the stares. I've considered taking a class, even visited Wednesday-evening Yoga, but performing both arm and leg exercises at the same time is difficult for me. Coordination is not my forte. I was always the kid who, in physical-education class, had trouble with the jumping jacks; as an adult, I would rather suffer embarrassment alone.

Like any hangout, the gym has its cliques, unspoken rules, and dress codes. Some people work out alone. Men tend, in my gym at least, to work out in twos or groups. They spot each other and argue about the Dolphins, the Heat, the Marlins. They wear baseball caps and wide leather belts to help their back muscles.

Women wear Spandex, in every imaginable color and pattern. One enthusiast must own at least a dozen workout outfits—each more interesting than the next. My favorite is her leopard print because she wears a matching scrunchy in her hair, an attention to detail that I find admirable. Some are perfectly groomed when they arrive to exercise, every hair in place and shorts the same color as the sports bra. They flee to the restroom in mid-workout to touch up their makeup. Obviously, perspiration is no excuse for looking sloppy. This single-minded effort has never failed to amaze me because I can barely dress myself before going to the gym. I roll out of bed and into my worn mesh shorts and even rattier tank top, brush my teeth and sometimes my hair, then stumble to the car. My husband, who accompanies me at that hour, does the same. I think, Why bother with physical appearance when you're sweating rivers? Wouldn't you look better sleeping ten minutes more anyway?

Like Spandex, water bottles are ubiquitous. You lift, you sip. You push, you sip. You pant, you sip. I can easily drink a liter or two of water during a one-hour workout. This is strongly encouraged by my former trainer because when I get home I sprint like a gazelle for the bathroom. Which means that I'm building my leg muscles, increasing my heart rate, and using up calories.

We see the same people week after week, and once in a while a few newcomers who venture in, try it out, then quit. The morning congregants know each other only by first name, if that. We trade stories, stock tips, weather reports: Conversations tend toward the impersonal. At one point, we suspected a romance in bloom, right there between the bench and the lateral rowing machine, but nothing came of it. Now the man and the woman rarely speak to each other. Still, the gym, I think, is a far better place to meet someone than, say, a bar or even the office. You know exactly what the person looks like at his worst: sweaty, heaving, frustrated, and exhausted.

I certainly am at my worst in the gym, namely because I can think of a million other things I'd rather be doing. I wince, grimace, frown, and squinch my face as I go through my routine. Just the other morning, a trainer who resembles the He-Man cartoon of my sons' childhood tried to cajole me into a smile. I told him I'd try, and I did—for about thirty seconds. There really isn't a lot to smile about at a gym, yet there are more than a reasonable amount of disconcerting moments. I, for one, find it unsettling to have a twenty-five-year-old with a flat stomach and narrow hips working out beside me. (Or worse, beside my husband.) It brings out this terrible little monster in my head that hisses: "Wait until she has children."

At the same time, in a gym I'm also at my best: working hard at something that goes against my nature but that I know is good for me. When I finish my routine, I feel a certain satisfaction at having stuck it out. What's more, because of cellulite, I can do things now that I couldn't do before.

I can open a spaghetti-sauce jar without anyone's help. I can lift several bags of groceries. I can run until nighttime without feeling frazzled and tired. I can pull myself onto the deck of our skiff from a chest-high ocean.

No small feats, these, but the exemplary accumulation of work and effort, struggle and perseverance. Wow!

Still, it would also be nice to have smooth, taut thighs.

Second Time Around

~~

We met at a party I had not planned to attend. A friend phoned to invite me on a Saturday evening when I was in the middle of a long writing session pressured by an imminent deadline. I declined. She insisted. The party was taking place in rural Miami-Dade County, an area of farms and orchards and cows that sometimes wander into the middle of dirt roads, and she did not want to venture there alone. I suggested alternatives. Then she pulled out her trump card.

"They're serving lobster," she told me matter-of-factly.

"Give me thirty minutes," I replied.

On that spring evening, it was unusually warm and muggy, the type of weather that frizzes hair and invites mosquitoes. I dressed accordingly: sleeveless pullover, worn golf skirt, repellent. I had no more than closed the door of my friend's car when I informed her: "You owe me big for this one." She laughed. Now I wonder if she sensed anything.

It is a long drive from the congestion and city lights of Miami to the dense darkness of Homestead, and I felt an uneasy guilt worming its way into my heart. My children were spending the weekend at their grandparents' so I could finish my work, but here I was, ready to waste precious time at a party where I wouldn't know a soul. Reading my thoughts, my friend promised me we wouldn't be long.

We pulled up to the driveway at about the same time a stranger was stripping off his leather gloves before positioning his helmet on the backrest of a Harley. He confirmed we were at the right place. Without looking back, my friend and I marched into the house, bearing a store-bought lemon pound cake and a bottle of white wine we would have opened on the drive there had we had a corkscrew.

The house sat in the middle of an acre of fruit trees. That night, the trees looked uncannily like giants having a bad-hair day, wild and unruly. Inside, a staircase that turned in on itself rose from the center of the living room. To the left, in the brightly lighted kitchen, a few women were setting out an entrancing collection of desserts on the counter. We entrusted the pound cake and the bottle of wine to one of them and headed for the wraparound porch, where most of the party goers were milling around tables laden with chips and an assortment of hors d'oeuvres. A television blared the hotly contested NCAA semifinal basketball game between Utah and North Carolina.

Later, the stranger would tell me that I walked right by him and, with a cursory glance, demanded: "Where's the lobster?"

"It's not ready," he claims he answered.

I don't remember the exchange.

As soon as she was spotted, my friend was whisked away by colleagues from the public school system. I hovered around the dip and chips, feeling abandoned. Perhaps sensing this, the stranger sidled up to me, beer in hand, and started up a conversation. We began by talking about fishing, then moved on to boating. Later, he admitted he was impressed by the fact that I was familiar with the kind of boat he owned—a twenty-foot skiff ideal for flats fishing. From there, we ventured to the more exploratory topic of jobs and career. He told me he had been teaching shop to special-education students at a nearby middle school for twenty-five years. I looked him over more closely and thought: Who the hell would do *that* for twenty-five years? And at a middle school! We segued into children. He had two. When I mentioned five, he did not walk away. I noticed that, with heels, I was taller than he was. Strands of white were woven in the blond and brown of his beard.

When the host proclaimed the lobster tails ready, we queued up in a noisy line of teachers, guidance counselors, program administrators, and assistant principals. The stranger had a name now—David. At a table in a dim corner of the porch, he took a seat beside me. We were soon joined by others. When it was David's turn to tell stories, his hand grazed mine, a light flirtatious touch. I noticed his forearms, thick and veined. Strong.

After dessert, when we were alone in a wooden swing, he asked for my phone number. I gave it to him with a list of conditions. He shouldn't call before nine p.m. because I was busy with my children, and I could not talk past ten-thirty, my bedtime. He asked me out. I didn't do weekdays, I added. He pushed for the following Friday. I turned him down. He asked if he could phone me Monday. I shrugged my approval.

On the way home, my amused friend warned me that this was the type of man who would do as he said. I figured he would just as soon forget. Besides, I did not want to complicate my life any more than necessary, and relationships, I had learned through trial and error, did precisely that. They took up time and emotional energy; at the slightest encouragement, they became complex entities that demanded more than I was willing to give.

David called Monday at lunch. Just to say hello. Before hanging up, he asked if we could continue the conversation that evening. We did. Tuesday we attended a reading by the well-known Latin American author Isabel Allende. The following night, we talked on the phone past two in the morning. Thursday, after he got off work, he asked to meet me for coffee. I went.

I left late that evening on a much-awaited trip with my children to Buenos Aires and Patagonia. That weekend, he went off alone on a leisurely motorcycle tour through some of the back roads of the South. Thousands of miles away, on opposing sides of the hemisphere, we couldn't stop thinking of each other. Upon my return twelve days later, we picked up right where we had left off. Our friends were taken aback by our uncharacteristic behavior. Cautious, deliberate, and far from impetuous, we were the two people considered the least likely candidates for a whirlwind romance. But then, preconceived notions don't matter much with love. Six months and six days after we met, we married.

I have told this story, as David has, countless times, and with every recounting I realize I remember something else about that first night in Homestead: the sound of the crickets or the taste of the tomato salad, the smell of barbecued corn, the glossy feeling of time holding still for a few hours, a bubble over a perfect moment. I supply these details in the ensuing telling because it adds veracity but also because listeners, eager for signs of lasting passion and mutual devotion, cling to portents of any kind.

Tales of how people meet comprise the mythology of love, the sweet hopefulness that balances out the bitterness of hard-fought endings. Beginnings are all about infinite possibilities, a temporary standoff with reality. And so, we long to hear about those first magical, unblemished moments to assure ourselves of both the power and the randomness of romance.

How did you meet? How did you meet? Parents ask this to make sure everything is on the up-and-up. Children ask because it is their way of piecing together the world of their parents before they themselves arrived or, in the case of second marriages, of figuring out where they fit in. And single people, the most attentive listeners of all, ask, analyzing, calculating, dissecting—and hoping, hoping that what happened once might happen again. To them.

Consider the proliferation of singles groups, happy hours, dating services, personal Web pages. The yearning to love and be loved is as old as time itself. We are forever seeking companionship, the care and trust of another soul. As a friend once noted wryly, we want to be important to somebody other than our mother, and we specifically want validation of a romantic sort. I call this need to couple off the Noah's Ark Syndrome. But despite its prevalence, we tend to mock this very human need because the pain of a failed relationship—and sometimes the agony of its success, too—can be so ravaging.

Still, we want it. Oh, how we want it! If my personal experience is typical, love arrives with stealthy steps and when you least expect it. It has an endearing way of slapping you on the back, grabbing you by the arm, swinging you around, and kissing you full on the mouth. When this happens, you leap right into it. At nineteen, I leapt with my eyes shut and heart open. At forty-one, I pushed off with eyes wide and heart scarred. A lifetime of experience had changed the way I reacted to the quick beating of my heart.

When you have loved and lost, as most of us have by the time we approach middle age, a protective crust of defensive behaviors fits snugly over the tender wound of experience. For a while, I preferred (with what I think is good reason) safety. I pushed away. I sabotaged. I used the children as shields. I employed work as an excuse. I refused to risk. But never say never. Such words come back to haunt you, and with a wild vengeance, too. Love is a siren's song, and our desire for it a powerful persuader. Everything I swore I wouldn't do a second time—too much trouble, too much uncertainty, too much grief—I did again.

By the time we hit forty, we've given up on fairy tales, though I dare say not always on the fairy-tale *endings*. Maturity tames us, sedates us, lowers our expectations. Yet, because we have grown familiar with loneliness, we are also more willing to recognize the importance of a good person in our life. I certainly was. For me, love the second time around was sweet and heavy and just plain refreshing, like a lick of honey from the refrigerator. It was as exhilarating, as silly, as encompassing as first love—but different. Experience had taught me to cherish the exhilaration, to recognize its preciousness.

Love in middle age has come with less flame and more gratitude, an unusual alchemy of passion and appreciation, hope and faith. The second time around has been not so much about correcting past mistakes as about the willingness to make new ones. I've lived long enough to regret actions committed in spite and words uttered in anger. I have become well versed in the sins of omission and accusations that have festered too long, and I know, too, that nothing is as arduous and time-consuming, nothing requires as much patience, compromise, and understanding, as keeping two people together, in love, and committed to each other.

But you know what? I'm sure I can do it, and I believe David can, too. That's the other thing about maturity. Not only have I become a more astute judge of character, but I know myself better, too: what I am willing to negotiate and what I can't possibly, under any circumstances, live with again.

Long before I knew David, a group of friends and I got together to attend a church workshop on relationships. Afterward, inspired by the talk, we camped out in one of the women's homes and, over wine and German chocolate cake, drew up individual lists of the ten qualities we expected from our mates. Two traits made it to the top three spots in each of our lists, and though we initially expressed amazement at this, we later agreed that the results were to be expected. All of us were in our thirties and forties and had been married at least once before. Our expectations were tempered with experience.

The two essentials we all listed? A sense of humor and good sex. Laughter and loving. And after further discussion, we also agreed that, on occasion, mixing the two is absolutely necessary. I would have never known that at nineteen.

The first time David asked me to marry him, about two months after we met, I was taken aback by his audacity. He had posed the question in an off-hand manner, more statement than inquiry. I answered with what I think is characteristic frankness—No way, Jose, or something to that effect. This did not discourage him, only taught him to bide his time. He claims he sensed an opening, a softening. I can't imagine how.

Marriage was not in my script. I had sworn up and down to friends and family that I wouldn't march to nuptials a second time. Not because I didn't have a good first marriage but because, still bruised by the grief of a husband's unexpected death, I wanted to devote myself to the business at hand: raising children alone. But God has a sense of humor, see. He let me plot and plan, devise all kinds of rules to protect my role as a single woman. Then He sent David to change the well-crafted scene—actually, the whole story-line.

When David finally got around to asking again, I was ready. We were in my living room, a place rarely used except by guests for formal visits, when he dropped to his knee and took my hand in his. "Yes! Yes! Yes!" I replied, and pulled him up to hug him. Every night now I thank God for that clever plot twist. I thank Him even on the days that David and I have argued or disagreed. That is another difference between loving in my forties and loving in my teens. I know that every valley must eventually surrender to a peak.

Friends were skeptical, however, and rightly so. A second marriage, I was warned, had none of the charming novelty of a first but plenty of obstacles. Children, mortgages, pets, investments, ex-spouses (alive or dead), and emotional hurts. History chases us. We are who we are because of what has happened to us, good and bad. Like so many survivors, David carried baggage from a failed first marriage, and I, I arrived with steamer trunks. (The memory of a dead man beloved by his wife and children haunts his family long after he has left them, and it takes a very strong, self-assured man to accept this.)

We had issues of lifestyle to contend with, too; still do. If the longevity of marriage is improved by the similarities between husband and wife, on the surface our situation surely seemed destined for failure. David and I come from disparate backgrounds and different religions. He's Jewish; I'm Catholic. He's Florida born and raised. I'm Cuban, raised here and there. We cook differently, we pray differently, we play differently.

"You're stepping up to the plate," a clergyman warned me, "with two strikes already called on you."

He wasn't exaggerating. But in the end, has it mattered? Yes and no. Ultimately, we can't imagine being without each other. That is not to say, however, that merging our lives has been smooth and peaceful, an expressway to bliss. Hardly. We've discovered pot-holes and ditches, a road that is more curves and hairpin turns than straightaway. There are times, when I wake at first light, that I stare at the man and miracle beside me and wonder how two people so unalike could agree so fiercely in their future together. I wonder if he doesn't harbor those same unsettling thoughts as I sleep next to him. (We sleep as we lead our lives, intermittently resting on oppo-site ends of the bed but then intertwining limbs, pressing bodies, reaching hotly for each other in the middle of the night.) There is a foreignness in him that is both appealing and frightening, and I am surprised by those thoughts, by that fear and the dividedness in me, because I know I cannot, will not, ever *ever* let him go. Yet, so much of him seems unreachable to me at times. I feel as though I've walked into the middle of a play and been told to take a leading role without having learned all the lines.

For him it must be doubly hard. David went from being single for ten years and living with his two children every weekend to a raucous household with five full-time children, all of whom were a bit leery of his intentions. He moved into *my* house with *my* kids and *my* rules and *my* decorations. He gave up his way of life, the very routine that had for so long defined his days. To state it so sim-ply, though, is to diminish the effort, the work, and, yes, even the resentment of the surrender. Sometimes I will find him in a corner of the living room—the room no one uses, the room in which he proposed—reading the mail or simply sitting alone. "Just need a lit-tle space," he explained the first time. I was alarmed by his behav-ior. What did it really mean? Was he having second thoughts? But the more he did it, the more I noticed the noise and activity level in the house. It was loud and busy and nonstop, like a college frater-nity. What a contrast to what he had known! That realization made me love him, and appreciate him, that much more.

Another thing about the second time around: I expect marriage, like romance, to be more a la carte than all-inclusive. David and I choose what we want to do together and what we prefer to do alone, without guilt or accusations. We have our separate interests, our separate friends, our separate bank accounts, even our own separate sets of kitchenware. Yet, I also spend more time with David than I have with any other man, and sometimes I do so with enormous, succoring gulps, defensively almost, and always with that undercurrent of fear . . . who knows, who knows. Having buried a husband at thirty-seven, I am suspicious of what tomorrow will bring, and doubt my ability and power to stop it.

If first marriages are about matching towels, good china, and starting a family together, I've discovered that a second marriage often turns out to be about scattered bits and mismatched pieces, furniture that doesn't go together, and two of almost everything for the kitchen. It is primarily about hope, Mr. Clergyman, about stepping up to the plate with two strikes and two outs in the bottom of the ninth, with a southpaw on the mound.

And believing against all odds that you're destined to hit it out of the ballpark.

Bugs in My Teeth

My husband is lying on just-laundered sheets, resplendent in the silk, zebra-print boxers I bought him during one of my wifely forays into a dreaded shopping mall. His muscled legs rest just so over a forest-green pillow, and the flat stomach he zealously works on every morning stretches hard and inviting to the ripple and curve of deltoids, biceps, shoulders. He smells of soap.

"David," I whisper into his ear, trying to imitate a sultry sound I've been told is irresistibly sexy.

He doesn't flinch. Outside, the evening rain plip-plops against the bedroom window, but he doesn't seem to hear it, so intent is he on reading. The magazine arrived in the mail this morning. On the cover, a woman stands next to a motorcycle, legs apart, staring into the camera with a come-hither look and two minuscule pieces of red fabric strategically placed over her body. Personally, I think she looks trashy.

"David," I repeat, this time louder.

"What? What?" he replies, startled. Then he looks at my bedtime outfit and smiles. He caresses my waist. "Honey," he says in that deep, gravelly voice that drives me wild, "would you look at this?"

Breathless, he passes me the magazine and turns to the center-fold, an enormous color photograph of a beauty in all its chrome splendor, a breathtaking collection of fine lines and steely curves: a restored Indian. He reads the motorcycle's specifications over my shoulders like a disciple reading his master's pronouncements, all awe and worship.

Some men look at naked women in magazines. My husband stares at photographs of bikes in the buff. The girl in the red bikini? Who cares! (Well, okay, he does peek, but for him, she's a mere prop.) He is vastly more interested in the chrome pipes, stainless-steel parts, plastic windshields, and assorted stuff sold in these magazines. Catalogs, he pants over. And why not? Read the lyrical descriptions of these machines and you will understand how words can send a virile heart soaring: *screamin' pipes . . . a true sculpture for the machine age . . . extraordinary work of art . . . anti-corrosion treatment . . . leather saddlebags and Plexiglas windscreen as standard . . . radical paint and chrome . . . easy-starting, oil-tight V-twin rumbling through its hardtail-style chassis . . . chrome tear headlamp . . . lustrous black finish.*

I know of husbands who, with just the right kind of inflection, recite poetry to their wives while snuggling in bed by candlelight. Blake, cummings, Whitman, Yeats. David, on the other hand, trills the specifications of a whole other kind of throbbing. Just the other night, mesmerized by a story in *Men's Journal* he read me a short piece written by Peter Fonda. In it, the movie star told about riding his motorcycle from his ranch in Montana south to Yellowstone National Park, then returning via Cooke City for some fly-fishing on Upper Clarks Fork before heading back home. At the end of the story, David sighed. Such longing in that expression.

David's is a quiet passion, a lover's tongue-tied, unassuming worship. Though he tries to ride whenever he can, occasionally a week or two might go by before he can hop on his bike and confront the wind. He suffers the separation in sulking silence. For David the Devotee, the love of motorcycles extends beyond the surface vr-r-room and vibration; it is more appreciation of engine turned art. And I don't mean this flippantly, either. David cannot walk past a bike—whether oil-specked or in high sheen—without stopping to admire its arch and bend, the height of its handlebars, the tilt of its seat. He can't help himself: His eyes are drawn to the hint of grease and dirt and defiance.

The obsession began in his youth, in simpler times, when he rode his friends' motorcycles. He bought his first one right out of college, at twenty-two, a Kawasaki 400. Why, I asked him, did he buy a bike if he was strapped for money and already had a car? He looked at me as if he didn't understand. I realized I was asking the wrong question. David bought the bike on a Friday, and the following morning rode down from Miami to Key West with a group of friends. Three or four years later, however, after he had married and his first wife wouldn't ride with him, he sold the Kawasaki.

For almost two decades, he was sorry he had done so.

There's still very much of the little boy in him. Well, maybe not the little boy, but the teenager who liked to hold his head high into the wind. To say, however, that riding a motorcycle is his way of recapturing lost youth is to reduce complex motivation to a simplistic bumper sticker: YOUNG AGAIN or BORN TO BE WILD. There are many more complicated reasons than the love of speed to rev up a Twin Cam 88 engine. For one, David rides to reduce stress. Helmeted, gloved, and booted, he can think of only one thing—the road ahead and nothing else. But he rides, first and foremost, because he loves it.

Several months after we met, after he had asked me for a photograph he could put on his desk at work, I decided I felt confident enough to ask for a return of the favor. I wanted, I told him, a picture or two that meant something to him. No cheesy studio portraits. I wanted him in his favorite clothes or at his favorite hangout, surrounded by something that chanted: This is David! This is David! It didn't take him long to figure out exactly what to give me. I received one snapshot of David on his flats boat, hands on the wheel, a straw hat on his head. In the second picture, he leaned against his bike packed for a road trip, grinning smugly into the camera. I had no reason to wonder what to expect from this man on his days off.

When we married, his son and best man thought long and hard about how he would bless his father's new beginning. He sought advice from a family friend, a biker like David who reveres exhaust pipes and cruising pegs. In his toast, Dylan urged us to ride into the sunset, "the wind in your face, the bugs in your teeth." Gee, I thought, while sipping champagne in my sprayed hairdo and gold heels, I've really got something to look forward to.

Now, at the foot of our bed, on two antique pine chests brought over from his house, he keeps an eclectic collection of bike books, totems to a religion he can practice not nearly as much as he would like. My favorites are illustrated histories, not because I prefer to look at pictures but because, as a writer, I know words cannot do justice to the angles and the lines, the gleam and the glint of these machines.

When we go to a bookstore, he invariably ends up not at the cafe ordering latte but browsing through yet one more tome to horse-power. There are so many! Where do all these glossy biker books come from? And who buys them at twenty, twenty-five dollars a pop anyway?

Bikers just like David, that's who. See, today's bikers are different than those of yesteryear's— or, at least, our image of yesteryear's pot-bellied, tattooed savages who roared into town, brawled at bars, and then hollered for their equally crude biker babes. The bikers I know are a more revised, literate edition of the Hell's Angels: a judge, a teachers union vice president, a housewife, an attorney, the in-house counsel for a utility company, a pet-cemetery owner, a realtor, a trainer, an insurance-company executive, a special-education teacher, a children's doctor, a stockbroker. They all have stock portfolios, mortgages, panel-lined offices, and country-club dues. They are also older, most likely married, better educated, and better off financially than enthusiasts of the past. In some circles, they are referred to as Rubbies, or rich urban bikers. Look at the cost of bikes and their accessories, and you'll understand why Rubbies need a healthy salary and a good credit line to be bad to the bone. There are a lot more women riding their own bikes, too—eight percent compared with one percent in the 1960s.

If you doubt the image change, consider a 1999 Progressive Insurance survey of 1,100 men, which revealed this startling fact: Bikers are (gasp!) soft. They are, for instance, five times more likely to cry during movies than nonbikers. They give flowers more often, are more moved by poetry, and want to be like Paul Newman and Oprah Winfrey. What's more, the most popular movie titles named by riders were, by and large, romances: *Shakespeare in Love, Jerry Maguire, The Prince of Tides,* and *Titanic.* The inspiring *It's a Wonderful Life* also scored high. On the other hand, the cult classic *Easy Rider* ranked only twenty-first. Imagine that.

Yet, it is the allure of speed and menace, of pure political incorrectness, that attracts these upscale guys and gals to thunder. There is a certain romantic recklessness, an unfettered fierceness, in riding down the road with no walls, with only the most basic protection. Even the disdain with which motorcyclists refer to their machine's prim and proper cousin, the automobile, as "cage" smacks of rebellion. They remember Marlon Brando in *The Wild One*, Arnold Schwarzenegger in *Terminator 2*, Malcolm Forbes in . . . Wait! The late, rich Malcolm Forbes? Yes, the very one. The millionaire motorcycle enthusiast is often credited with powering these chrome beauties into the affluent mainstream. He was helped, of course, by various respectable publications, including business magazines that told their readers that motorcycles "hold their value." Incredible! Value appreciation and in-your-face excitement, truly an investment for the twenty-first century.

Motorcycles are so legitimate that the Guggenheim in New York City, a museum designed to exhibit the world's great collections of modern art, put on display one hundred and fourteen specimens of metal and motor sculpture the very summer I began riding with David. It attracted record crowds and critical acclaim. The introduction on the Guggenheim web site explained why motorcycles belonged, at least temporarily, in an art museum: "The motorcycle is an immortal cultural icon that changes with the times. More than speed, it embodies the abstract themes of rebellion, progress, freedom, sex and danger."

Immortal cultural icon.

Abstract themes.

Rebellion, progress, freedom, sex, and danger.

And I thought of them as wheels with a little chrome thrown in for effect!

David owns a Harley-Davidson 1993 Dyna Wide Glide. For as long as I've known him, he has been seriously considering purchasing another one because . . . well, because two Harleys are better than one. On the days the Harley shop near our home puts the bikes out for test drives, he spends a Saturday morning there, riding a Softail, a Fat Boy, a Low Rider—any and every Harley available. He returns home with a full recounting of exhaust pipes, engine pickup, seat comfort, handlebar height, and overall beauty. Most of the time I have no idea what he is talking about, though I've noticed that, like him, I now turn my head to check out a bike when it whizzes by us.

A friend whose husband spends all his free time building and flying model airplanes advised this when I married: "You can fight it and be miserable, or you can join him and learn to like it."

I joined. Now I ask ignorant questions about motorcycles he lusts after. I accompany him on runs. I attend biker parties. He may never buy a second bike, but it won't be because I told him not to. If he does buy one, though, I'm sure it will be another Harley. He admires Japanese imports, known haughtily, if insensitively, in some circles as "rice burners," but he prefers Harleys, the granddaddy of them all. "There are motorcycles, and there are Harleys," says David. For the most part, rice burners are faster and more modern in design. They come in racing trim, with aerodynamic windscreens and molded fairings to push the airflow around your legs. They look like they belong in a sci-fi flick.

Nice, all right, but they are not Harleys. Harleys as in Live to Ride, Ride to Live. Harleys as in Buy American. Harleys as in customize, customize, customize. Harleys hark back to the bad old days. They are what our parents warned us against. They've got class, style, heft. They make lots of vroom-vroom noise. More important, they possess The Mystique—and zealots willing to pay for it. Many cost as much as a cage and, true to their fair-prize-hog status, are B-I-G.

I can't think of any other form of transportation that inspires such frenzied devotion. People tattoo Harley insignia on their bodies, for chrissakes, and spend indecent amounts of money on Harley jackets, shirts, patches, bandannas, vests, caps, scarves, helmets, gloves, bags, boots, jewelry, you-name-it. Some even buy the stock.

Which leads me to a brief but necessary discussion of biker haute couture, where one fashion truism holds: What you wear is almost as important as what you ride. This means you gotta, just gotta, wear leather, preferably studded, fringed, and buckled. But rugged. And black. Ah, yes, always black.

This is one scene in which good guys wear black.

I was sixteen the first time I rode a motorcycle. A friend of my older brother's came by with his bike and asked if I wanted to hop on. Didn't have to think about it twice. Without helmet or parental permission, we motored around the block at a stately pace. The wind whipped my hair and the vibration massaged my legs, and I thought it was a little like riding a bicycle downhill fast. My mother grounded me as soon as I got home.

That was the extent of my pig-iron experience until I was forty-one years old. Quite frankly, I did not have the slightest interest in riding around with the roll of thunder between my legs. The wide roads and big skies did not call me. People who drove motorcycles, I thought, couldn't afford to own a car.

Then I met David—and his Harley. Three weeks later, on a cloudless Sunday afternoon, he came by the house to take me for a spin. My children greeted him with crossed arms and stern stares. It was only the second time they had seen him, and he was dressed to ride. Embarrassed, I rushed him out the door. They followed.

They spotted the bike. They uncrossed their arms, softened their stares.

"Is that a Harley?" my eldest son asked.

Not one to miss an opportunity, David began to show off his metal sculpture. The younger children circled the motorcycle and gingerly reached out to touch it. They spoke to each other in hushed tones, defensiveness having surrendered to reverence. Finally I squirmed into a helmet and David adjusted the strap. He had already warned me to wear long sleeves and long pants, boots or sneakers to cover my ankles. He mounted; I pretty much staggered on.

"When are you bringing her back?" my eldest son asked.

David gave him a time. We waved goodbye and left them, if not in the dust, in the fresh cuttings of just-mowed suburban lawn.

David later said he would never forget the look on my children's faces as they lined up on the porch to see a man on a motorcycle take their mother away. I was far from an exemplary passenger that first ride, holding him so tight he thought his ribs would crack. I naively pointed out the danger of riding a motorcycle, particularly in Miami's hellish traffic.

"Who said life was supposed to be safe?" he challenged me. "Life is all about risks."

He admitted later that he was talking about more than motorcycle riding.

Over time, with David's patient guidance, I learned to jerk around less and hold him more loosely. Sometimes I accompanied him to the Harley store and watched how his eyes grew wide, his fingers eager, when he looked at the display of pipes. We attended parties where grown men, and a few women, with all the material trappings of success, pined aloud for that vacation they would soon take on their bikes—the scenic New England tour, the cross-country to Maine, the back roads of the Old South. I didn't get it. What was the big deal? To be one with nature, I can sit out on the lawn chair in my backyard.

I am a good wife, though, and I love my husband and, as necessary, his toys. For Hanukkah, I gave him a Harley-Davidson lunch box and a collection of temporary tattoos. I began to read the newsletter from the local H.O.G. group—the factory-sponsored Harley-owners group. I stopped worrying about helmet hair and began noting the change in design among manufacturers, the way handlebars are set, and the distance between floor and pegs.

I am a firm believer that one should take an interest in the interests of loved ones. When my sons took up football, I learned football. When my daughter went through her brief Megadeth phase, I learned about metal music. The least I could do was immerse myself in motorcycles. I would do this for my husband. And I would do this because—hey, I'm actually curious about taking a ride on the wild side.

About six months into our marriage, David suggested I take a motorcycle-rider instruction class. His son, he said, had enrolled in the weekend course the year before, at fifteen, and had become a much better rider. I thought about it for a few months, then signed up with one of his friends, a school psychologist who, like me, wanted to be a better passenger on her husband's Harley. We thought ourselves wise and daring, in a wifely way.

Of the twelve students in the class, we were the only ones who had never driven a motorcycle. We were also the oldest. Having always owned cars with automatic transmissions, I knew nothing about clutches and gearshifts. During breaks in class that first night, the others excitedly discussed the bikes they owned or the ones they were about to buy. One guy, in his early twenties, bragged about the speeding accident he had survived. Another admonished him for his recklessness. A young woman, taking the class with her husband, had been racing dirt bikes since she was a girl. She wanted, she admitted, something tamer now. Listening to the details of their infatuations was like walking in on one of those infamously obsessive *Star Trek* conventions, but with bikers having replaced the Trekkies. I felt like an alien.

The following morning, each class member was assigned a motorcycle—my friend and I got red Honda 125s, everyone else the larger Honda 250—and we began to practice very basic exercises on the range. These included everything from how to walk beside the bike, to how to turn it on and keep the engine running. It was very intimidating, and my hands shook as I tried to concentrate on the instructions. By the third hour of this, my friend declared in a sotto voce whisper, "I hate it! I hate it!" She refused to participate in the drills and watched from the shade of a canopy. I chugged along. Actually, I twitched along, holding up the class, eliciting sighs from the instructors, and generally making a klutzy nuisance of myself. But I learned. I learned to swerve and weave, stop on a dime, take a sharp curve, hop over a log, do figure eights. Every time I finished an exercise, I thought: *Hey! Lookee me!* I didn't particularly like what I was doing, but I wasn't going to quit, absolutely not. I had paid one hundred and seventy-five dollars for the three-day course and, dammit, I was going to get my money's worth. When I finally graduated, completing my license examination at the end, an excited David gushed about buying me my own bike. I was silent. I didn't mind roaring off into the sunset tucked behind my husband, but zooming down a straightaway by myself . . . that was a different matter. There was the element of fear, of course—fear of danger and fear of my own incompetence—but my reluctance went beyond that. I had learned the basic hows of riding, but I had yet to fully understand the whys.

Months have passed since the motorcycle instruction course. David enlarged photographs of me riding the class Honda on the practice range. I look, strangely enough, as if I'm in control—and comfortable. There is no visible sign of my white-knuckle death grip or how, every day after class, I spent the evening flexing my hands to prevent cramps from that powerful grip.

He showed the snapshots to my father, who nearly fainted with the knowledge that his oldest daughter was courting danger with such open disdain. "A second adolescence, is this?" he admonished me in his quirky English. I informed David he wasn't racking up any points with his in-laws. At a family reunion, the photos were passed around to cousins from the Heartland and two other continents. Reactions were diverse, but divided generally along gender lines. The men wanted details; the women were flabbergasted.

"It takes a special kind of love," one cousin told me, shaking her head.

A love for what? I wondered. For a husband? For a motorcycle? For the satisfaction of doing something you could not once imagine doing?

I am told that the attraction of motorcycles, for women especially, is a slow burn. You don't ever see a girl steering an imaginary race car during second-grade recess, but by the time she becomes a teenager, the danger of speed, the speed of danger, can be as seductive as the bad boy next block over. Even in these increasingly egalitarian times, however, few of us women take up driving a motorcycle or plane or boat or hot rod without the influence of a husband or boyfriend. Certainly that is my case.

I still belong in a cage, the safety of metal between me and asphalt, but I would consider donning helmet and revving my own engine on one condition: the bike be outfitted with training wheels. Chrome, of course.

The Religion of Love

It began, as all good things should, in the kitchen. There was no rit-ual cleaning of countertops, no scouring of the oven, no hunt for im-proper food, the wayward chametz. None of this, no. But there were walnuts and apples, red wine and honey. And David at the food processor making the charoset. A few feet from him, just across the room, I stood with my head bowed, intent on following a spinach-soufflé recipe from a cookbook I had bought a few months earlier. It was one of the few dishes I would contribute to the evening's holiday meal, and I had chosen it for a very good reason: It was simple enough for me not to mess up. Above the din of the whirring blades, David began to reminisce about past Passovers, the kind of childhood mem-ories that come alive at the first waft of a particular food. I looked up from my book to listen to the stories—about Elijah, about his father's bar mitzvah goblet put out for the prophet, about his grandmother's homemade horseradish, and about the boisterous search with his brother and sister for the hidden *afikomen*—and I realized how very different the details of our holiday memories were, yet how alike, too. Though his Passover and my Easter have had a tumultuous and often bitter coexistence, they share the celebratory qualities of family and food. Maybe all religious holidays do, regardless of origin or belief.

That day, the second of Pesach, we spent dicing, slicing, marinating, stirring. Roasting lamb scented the kitchen and matzo-ball soup bubbled on the stove. At times, I felt like a stranger in my own home. I had been a guest at other Passover Seders, the last one at my sister-in-law's the night before, but I had never been the hostess or the part-time cook. I wasn't sure what to do. Rifling through the refrigerator and the pantry for ingredients, it occurred to me that both storage areas reflected the resulting hodgepodge of a marriage between a Cuban Catholic and an American Jew: the jar of gefilte fish two shelves above the sliced ham for school lunches, the box of matzo next to the crusty loaf of Cuban bread, potato starch near the cans of black beans, pareve margarine with a brick of guava paste. Love makes for strange shelf-fellows.

David and I set the table together, a wineglass at every place and an extra one near the center for the famous prophet who manages to visit every household—even, I suppose, the ones of interfaith couples. This was more than a simple goblet, though. It was David's silver bar mitzvah cup, like his father's before him, and he set it in place with ceremonious tradition. He also positioned Seder plates on either side of the long table, each with its roasted shankbone, hard-boiled egg, horseradish, charoset, and parsley. At his corner, he wrapped the matzos in a cloth. As night fell and guests gathered and candles were lighted, flickering flame and glowing chandelier were refracted in our glasses. Of all the foreign holidays becoming familiar to me, I realized this was perhaps the one I liked best. Passover is the great festival of liberation, the commemoration of the Israelites' freedom from the bondage of Egypt. As the offspring of a family that has suffered political bondage of some kind for several generations, I can identify with that freedom and that search for it.

Sitting on a hardback chair in the formal dining room, David began with the Kiddush, the blessing. We followed from the deluxe edition of the Haggadah, distributed by Maxwell House. We sipped our wine. (When the kids grimaced, we replaced one fruit of the vine with another, grape juice.) In silence we washed, pouring water from a ceramic jar, right hand first, then left, three times. David plucked the parsley in front of him, dipped it in salt water, and continued: *Baruch atah Adonai, Elohaynu melech ha-olam Boray P'ree ha-adamah.* Blessed art thou, O Eternal, Our God, King of the Universe, Creator of the fruits of the earth. He broke the middle matzo in two, leaving one half between the two whole ones and putting the other half under a cloth. Lifting the matzos, he recited another passage, this one about the bread of affliction and ancestors in the land of Egypt.

Then came the moment for the children to shine. David prompted the youngest person present—in this case, we cheated and allowed the second youngest—to ask the four questions. The other children were fascinated by the solemnity of the moment. In fact, they remained quiet through most of the ceremony. When young stomachs grumbled with hunger, though, we rushed through the Haggadah, stopping at the places David considered appropriate, particularly the tasting of the horseradish, which was spit out immediately and cleared away with great gulps of water.

Finally, just as the children were growing antsy, we served the holiday meal on the good china: first the colored jewels of fruit, then the hard-boiled egg slip-sliding away in saltwater broth, the chicken soup with matzo balls and floating soup nuts, and the slab of gefilte fish in its broth. My children picked at the offerings, suspicious of the tastes and texture of this bounty. (Certainly there are foods that require a familiarity to be enjoyed, gefilte fish being one. Others, such as matzo-ball soup, had already become a permanent part of our year-round menu.) Later, after the day's work had been consumed in the blink of an eye by the famished family, when the fourth and final glass of wine was raised, and as David's voice rose above the murmurs with the ancient words *Baruch atah Adonai . . . ,* I looked down the long table at my Catholic children and their Catholic friends and knew they would never forget their first Seder. Others would follow but none would be like the first. Eventually, from these festivities they would glean the special knowledge of a history beyond the Bible, the history that gave rise to their own.

They would learn that the lamb bone symbolizes the animal sacrifices of early Hebrews, the charoset the mortar of the pyramids, the awful horseradish the bitterness of bondage, the parsley all our new beginnings, the unleavened matzo the haste of the slaves fleeing.

And they would know, too, that the Last Supper was, first and foremost, a Passover Seder.

Three days later, on our first Good Friday as a married couple, I was back in the kitchen after a Stations of the Cross service at my parish. In keeping with Lenten restrictions, I avoided red meat and prepared a simple but special meal for the family: lobster tails, drawn butter, corn pudding, and tossed salad. Matzo, too, of course. All afternoon, while humming in the kitchen, I had imagined the look of surprised delight on David's face when he spotted one of his favorite dishes. But when we finally sat down to eat and I served the meal with the appropriate fanfare, David's face displayed something quite different.

"Lobster? We're having lobster?" he mumbled.

I nodded eagerly.

"I can't eat it."

"You sick?" I could not imagine any other reason.

"It's shellfish."

Those two words slammed me like a dozen coconuts to the head. I felt welded in my seat, embarrassed, mortified beyond words. Though he was quick to comfort, the pleasure of the moment had passed. No matter how much David tried to ease the situation, I couldn't help but wallow in the misery of my indiscretion. I had lost my appetite. Finally, my middle son, probably exasperated by the delay in the meal, leaned over to David and said, "Hey, if you're not eating it, can I have the lobster?" I brought out leftover gefilte fish, and thus it was settled.

I told a friend about that awkward scene a few days later. She is Jewish, and half of an interfaith household. "It's just the beginning," she warned, laughing. Then she reminded me of the movie *The Jazz Singer* when, in the remake, Lucy Arnaz serves Neil Diamond a glistening baked ham. Knowing I had company alleviated the embarrassment only slightly. I remained frightened at what lay ahead of me.

When David and I decided to marry, the matter of religion inevitably came up. Did I have a problem, he asked, with the fact that he was Jewish? I replied honestly, an answer that will remain forever true in my heart: I would have problems only if he did not believe in God. We knew enough about each other's religion to understand that there were many similarities but also, at times, an abyss of differences and, among our peoples, centuries of mistrust. Yet, we agreed that our faiths, and the rites and rituals that came with the expression of those faiths, were an essential part of our lives. Neither of us wanted to convert and each was intent on impressing that on the other. We knew who we were, how we were raised, and the way we wanted to remain. Had we been younger and at another stage in our lives, had we wanted more children, the issue of religion would surely have been stickier, the discussion more heated. We both knew interfaith couples still arguing, so many years later, about how to raise the kids: Baptism or bris? Confirmation or bar mitzvah? Christmas or Hanukkah? Easter or Passover? The children ended up being raised with no religion at all. We would not have to face that. On the outside chance that we became parents again, David wanted to follow his own religion's matriarchal mandate: Raise children in the faith of their mother. This is what we were doing already, anyway. David's children from his first marriage had been raised Jewish. Though their mother was Jewish, their religious upbringing had been primarily David's doing. Mine were being brought up in their parents' faith under my tutelage, with all the pomp of the Catholic Church.

Still, issues of this type are not so easily resolved in a night of discussion, and we knew well that matters of how we pray and what we preach have long divided nations. Surely, a marriage can fall victim to the same rhetoric, the tireless self-righteousness that has brought down entire civilizations. We were adamant that we did

not want that for ourselves. Instead of concentrating on what separated us, we chose to focus on what we could share: the comfort
and gratitude of believing in the same Creator. In theory, it is a
commendable pursuit. In practice . . . in practice, it takes practice.
Quickly, David and I learned that it's the balancing of the details—
Passover gefilte leading to Good Friday lobster, Hanukkah candles
in one room and the Nativity in another—that tries our private
commitment to our religions and to our marriage. Unlike similar
couples in other eras, we did not face outright ostracism from our
families or our places of worship. Prejudice, in this politically correct age, is less obvious and more subtle. What we discovered instead was plenty of ignorance, even within ourselves, about who we
were and what we believed in, as well as a bureaucratic resistance
by some clergy to understand the religion of love.

In the beginning, I was concerned about the reaction of his family. Besieged by an intermarriage rate of more than fifty percent,
American Jews worry about their children marrying outside the
faith. To preserve the religion, they counsel marrying their own. A
friend I had known for years explained her encouragement of her
son's romances this way: "I can't pick whom he's going to fall in
love with, but I sure can facilitate the kind of girls he's going to
meet when he's ready to get serious." In other words, in words I
had heard before and not always in jest: Shiksas are for practice.

I knew that David's family, though far from Orthodox, was fairly
observant. His parents had kept kosher when he was a baby, and
now his sister's family did, too. An uncle two counties north of us
was a rabbi. David, though not a weekly-services kind of guy, was
active in Havurah of South Florida, a congregation that seeks to
move the religion back into people's homes. When I met him, he
was on the Havurah board and had been voted incoming president.
With his yarmulke and prayer book, he attended weekly groups
and studied Kaballah. Where would I fit in this world? Certainly
going to the bar mitzvahs of friends' children was not enough
preparation.

We decided to attend a Wednesday study group together. The

subject was right down our alley: sex, love, and marriage. We met at his rabbi's house, in a group small enough to gather around the dining-room table. For four weeks, I listened carefully. I recognized some of the teachings—the same underpinnings of my own religion—but the foreignness of the Hebrew grated on my ears. A product of Catholic schools, where we learned dogma without much attention to meaning, I was bewildered by the arguing—actually, by the encouragement of the arguing, the need for questioning.

Together, we also went to other functions of Havurah: to High Holy Day Services, to Shabbat dinners, to meetings with a well-known rabbi. I met David's family, individually then all together on Rosh Hashanah eve. Never did I feel unwelcome. If there were any grumblings, I didn't hear them. I did, however, sense a curiosity about my family and culture, my own religion, and how much I knew of the religion I was marrying into. An unspoken question seemed to hover in the air: Do you really know what you're getting into? At Havurah, several members confided that their own children had married Christians. One man told me about his conversion to Judaism. In the end, though, it came down to this: We're glad to see David happy.

My family proved to be more skeptical. Or maybe it was only that I was privy to that cautious skepticism. At one point, my father told me, "When you convert, I hope you will still raise the children Catholic." I had never mentioned any intentions of this kind. On the contrary, I had been very up front about not converting. Once those fears were allayed, my family then began posing tentative questions: Had I enrolled the children in Sunday school again? Would Ben be doing his First Communion? Was I still going to Mass? Would Christopher be confirmed the following year? As time passed, the inquiries slowed.

David participated in my religion, too. On occasional Sundays, he attended Mass with me. He enjoyed certain gospel stories, developed a taste for the sermons of a particular priest. He was amazed at how my religion resembled, in ritual at least, the old religion of his biblical ancestors. He also met members of the women's church group I belonged to. All had married within the religion and their spouses were active in the parish, so David immediately became a source of speculation. The curiosity I had encountered at Havurah was mirrored in the twice-monthly meetings at the homes of my church girlfriends.

I was not content, however, to leave well enough alone. I prodded and probed, insisted and persisted. It was as much to still the concerns in my mind as to discover the reality of his. Wouldn't he have preferred, I kept asking David, a Jewish woman? Someone who knew the prayers to recite before the lighting of the candles, the food to serve for the breaking of the fast after Yom Kippur, the song to sing at the end of Passover? Wouldn't he, wouldn't he?

Finally, one day, in exasperation, he replied: "It would have been easier, not better."

Easier, though, was not something either of us had chosen.

These words proved prophetic when it came time to marry. We met with his rabbi, who explained why, under Jewish law, he could not officiate at our wedding: As a gentile, I was not bound by the laws of Moses. There could be no *huppa*, the traditional marriage canopy, or *ketuba*, marriage contract. I knew David was disappointed, but we had suspected as much. Though friends had suggested names of rabbis who officiated at interfaith marriages, we did not feel comfortable seeing anyone other than David's rabbi and good friend. Besides, David's disappointment was ameliorated somewhat when the rabbi said he would be delighted to welcome the union by blessing our ceremony. It was a compromise that suited us.

On we went to my parish, and there it became incredibly complicated. To marry in the Catholic Church, the religion of a spouse does not matter as long as you agree to raise your children in the church. The status of a previous marriage does matter, however. Because I was widowed, I was free to remarry, but David, long divorced, was not. He needed an annulment, a process by which the church dissolves previous marital ties. This would take an average of eighteen months, though I knew of some that had been granted in half the time. We weren't willing to wait. Ultimately, though, it was not the time element that was such a stumbling block for either of us. It was the concept of annulment itself. We studied the literature my parish provided, met with a deacon I had long admired, and spoke to friends who had gone through it. David remained uncomfortable with the idea. And honestly, so did I. I could not understand how my church could recognize David's marriage in another faith but not his *get*, a religious divorce decree granted by a rabbinic tribunal. Why one and not the other? I argued. Where was the justification? What was the logic? I discussed the issue not only with representatives of my own parish, but with members of my family who were Eucharistic ministers and with an acquaintance who worked at the archdiocese. Their answers did not satisfy me. What's more, we could not persuade any priest (including my brother's uncle-in-law) to offer a blessing, in the same manner David's rabbi planned to do. The archdiocese frowned on any wedding ceremonies outside a church building.

As the fruitless search for a priest to bless us wore on, David told me he was willing to investigate the annulment process if it was the only way I could live with myself and with him. He would do it, he added, with great reluctance; his biggest concern was his children's reaction. But by then, after much internal wrestling, it was I who was not willing to go through the process. In my heart, the heart that loved a man, and in my soul, the soul that worshipped the Divine, I refused to believe that my God would not have blessed a marriage born of so much devotion. It struck me as a great cosmic joke that my church, founded by a Jewish carpenter and fisherman who also taught the masses, would deny me the blessing to marry a Jewish man, a teacher by training, and a carpenter and fisherman by vocation.

The religions' reaction to our interfaith wedding was relatively mild compared to segments of the self-righteous public. When I wrote a newspaper column about the blending of two families, Jew and Christian, readers were divided into very distinct camps: the liberal few who applauded what we did and the sanctimonious many ready to cast the first stone. Both sides quoted from the Bible.

"There is no salvation outside the Catholic Church," one wrote, "so you should try to convert your husband and his children. You must believe in the Messiah, Jesus Christ, or burn forever in hell. So stop spreading heresy."

That, thankfully, was balanced a bit with stories from children who had celebrated dual holidays in mixed marriages. "We not only received Christmas gifts under the tree but also Hanukkah gelt on the branches! It was always a special treat to go to temple with my cousins . . . I served as an altar boy every morning when I was young. On Sundays we would go to Mass, then over to my grandparents' for kosher lunch."

We were finally married by a neighbor, a criminal-court judge, and our union blessed by David's rabbi. No priest attended. Though hurt by my church's rigidity, I have continued participating in parish activities, taking Communion, and sending my children to Sunday school. Together, David and I have learned to navigate the dual-religion waters without compass but with a lot of trust—in God and in each other. I think we are doing a commendable job, moving beyond tolerance to acceptance and understanding. There are times, though, when I crave the comfort of an adult echoing the familiar liturgical phrases next to me in church. Once or twice a year, as the parish announces its Marriage Enrichment Program or its Couples Retreat Weekend, I long to participate with friends. I imagine he nurses yearnings of a very similar sort. On occasion, doubts run deeper still. In the solitude of prayer, that communion between self and Other, I can't help but wonder if for the sake of love on earth I have not forsaken a love of another kind, one of more permanence and greater importance. Have I—have we, David and I—lied to ourselves for the fulfillment of the moment? Have we fashioned God to suit our needs?

I think not. I cannot imagine God, a Father of forgiveness and acceptance, allowing religion to serve as an obstacle to love. From the Gospel of John (13, 31–33): "I am giving you a new command.

You must love each other, just as I have loved you. If you love each other, everyone will know that you are my disciples."

From friends, we learned that interfaith couples face two major stumbling blocks: over how to raise the children and over how to celebrate the holidays. The former had been decided for us by our past; the latter we decided to do equitably. In other words, we would celebrate his-and-hers holidays, and maybe an "ours" would come along. So, we decided to invite David's brother, sister, and father to my Christmas celebration—which is how, by default, we began a new tradition. Because his family does not eat pork—a braised pork leg is a staple of the Cuban *Nochebuena* (Christmas Eve dinner)—we supplemented the offerings with a roasted leg of lamb. We learned soon enough to be generous with the lamb. At our first Christmas as newly marrieds, we were caught unprepared. When my family realized there was lamb, they forgot all about the pork. It quickly dawned on us that we were now feeding both sets of relatives with the food we had expected to be consumed by half the guests. In a moment of panic, David grumbled, "I'm ready to carve the bone." I couldn't help but think about how Jesus had multiplied the loaves.

To the outside world, we appear to lead contradictory lives. We have been accused of secularizing our religions, of confusing our children, of perverting and tempting the other with false beliefs. What those critics don't see is that loving and living with someone who practices a religion other than mine has deepened my faith. It has prompted me to dig deeper within my own soul to understand what I have for so long done simply by rote. I know that my questions—Why do you . . . ? or Why can't you . . . ?—also give David pause. Worshipping with David has made me look beyond what I take for granted. It has helped me to separate religion from faith, piety from spirituality, human interpretations of divine mysteries from the reality that we cannot possibly conceive of certain things or of everything. The concept of God is so vast and our own ability to grasp Him so pitifully limited that more and more I am beginning to recognize that many roads lead to Him, roads I have not walked, roads I cannot claim.

My children's lives have been enriched in a way mine never was. And I'm not talking here about the suddenly popular idea of embracing diversity. This is about something deeper and wider and longer, about meaning and identity and awe, about the need we have to connect with God. For most of us, religion is not a choice but a birthright. We are born into one, and there we usually remain. The choice tends to come only in how much we truly practice what we preach. In my family, a family of exiles, we stuck to "our" people, "our" ways, "our" neighborhoods, "our" churches. We rarely knew of others' spiritual lives and longings. But in today's world, boundaries are flexible, interests expandable. My youngest children are being raised Catholic with a Jewish stepfather. They attend a school with classmates who are Muslim. They ask questions of me, of their stepfather, that I would never have known to ask at their age.

"If Jesus was Jewish and you are Jewish, why don't you believe in Jesus?"

"What do Jews believe in?"

"Are Christians Catholics, too?"

"Do you like the Pope?"

"What's inside that thing there [the Mezuzah on our door]?"

"What religion would Jesus have been if he had been born today?"

"Will you go to heaven if you're not Catholic?"

"What religion is God?"

These are questions that go to the heart of what we profess. Not only are they valid, but—with children especially—quite necessary. Faith, I think, is not built on ignorance but on belief that goes beyond the facts, beyond what we can see and hear and smell and touch. It should be a gate waiting to open, not a trapdoor to be held shut. Sometimes we find the qualities we treasure in the people who, at first glance, seem to be opening a gate different from ours. I tried to explain this during a rambling conversation about husbands with the women in my church group. I told them that what I loved most about David was his kindness and generosity, his readiness to forgive, his desire to help, the gentle way he deals with the less fortunate: the very same qualities Christ preached.

There is no getting around the central fact that I believe in Jesus as the Messiah and that David, my husband, the man with whom I have chosen to spend my life, thinks otherwise. There are differences one can't reconcile. Yet, in trying to do so, this is what I have discovered: How we live our lives, how we love our God, and how we care for our neighbor are more important than the church or synagogue where we choose to pray.

For weeks, Benjamin and I had been practicing the prayers he needed to know for his First Communion. David could hear my little boy's voice reciting the Act of Contrition and the Creed nightly, interrupted here and there with maternal corrections: *I believe in one God, the Father, Creator of heaven and earth. I believe in Jesus Christ, the only Son of God, who died and is risen for us. I believe in the Holy Spirit, the Lord, the giver of life. . . .* Sometimes after finishing with Benjamin, I would try to explain to David the process and preparation that leads to a young child's Communion. As Jesus' last Passover Seder, communion is easy to understand. On the other hand, Penance, or confession, is a trickier matter. What kind of horrible sins can an eight-year-old have committed? David asked. Why do you need an intermediary to speak with God? Do you go to Heaven regardless of how awful you've behaved during your life as long as you believe and ask forgiveness on your deathbed? What about the people who don't believe in Jesus Christ as the Messiah but have led exemplary lives? David's questions zeroed in on the differences in our religions, their very disparate outlooks on redemption and the afterlife.

On the February morning Benjamin was due in church with his classmates for his First Penance ceremony, I was in a nursing home with his grandmother, my first husband's mother. She had died a few hours earlier, a peaceful passage that had lifted a world of worry from my shoulders. Busy signing papers and finalizing details, I asked David to accompany my eight-year-old to confession.

"Ben," he joked with his stepson when he woke him, "you need something to tell the priest. We've got to do some serious *sinning* in the next hour and a half."

Benjamin giggled—precisely the reaction David wanted on this particular Saturday.

Three months later, during that sacred moment of his First Communion, David and I led him to the altar where he received the Host from a priest and placed it on his tongue.

"Are you still Jewish?" he later asked David, who had stood to one side when I approached the priest for my wafer.

"Are you still Catholic?" David teased back, without missing a beat.

Benjamin's Communion was followed by a meal at our house. We served brisket and rice and beans, conscious not to mix dairy and meat. During a breather at that gathering, David and I counted the number of family members who attended. We realized there were more Jews than Christians celebrating my little boy's big day, and as we sipped from a white wine designated kosher, we shared a private chuckle and wondered if anyone else had noticed. Surely God had and, in His infinite wisdom and with His inexplicable ways, was enjoying His own laugh.

Small Tomatoes

We have had a spat, David and I. We have argued and quarreled and turned our backs on each other, so now I can do little but think of our . . . our disagreement. Yes, let's call it that—a *disagreement*. Labeling it a *fight* makes it seem more violent and final.

I phoned him at work to blame him for my inability to get anything accomplished. He wasn't sympathetic. "So," he suggested, "write about it." He said it would be interesting to read something about the way couples fight, something that is human and real and as far from a Psychology 101 textbook as a Danielle Steele novel. The bit about the novel, he didn't say. I added that. I always have to get the last word in.

I think of fights, real fights, as screaming-insulting-hurling-everything-but-the-kitchen-sink episodes. You know the kind. Maybe you've been in them. I have. Not with David, though. I've never really thrown anything, either. Slammed a door, yes, but never ever hurled an object at a man. I've also said my share of horrible things I would like to take back. But we don't get giant erasers when we dive into a relationship. We don't get much of anything, actually, but hope, and hope is such a fragile thing.

David and I do not fight too long or too often or in too vicious a way. David is a negotiator and a diplomat. He does not get angry easily, and rarely at me. When he does, he expresses it in coherent sentences in a collected voice with calm gestures, and then he lets it go.

He lets it go. Can you believe that?

I simmer. I sauté. Then I boil over with great big, thick heaves, like a cheese-and-tuna casserole that's overflowed its dish. When this happens, I have trouble making sense. Occasionally, I mix my languages. I even curse. *Fuck off!* I snapped at him in our last . . . misunderstanding. This phrase was so unfamiliar to my lips that I think I mispronounced it. It sounded more like *duck, duck, goose.* He got my drift in spite of this.

The worst thing about fighting with David is that he does exactly what I tell him. If I hiss, "Get out of bed. I can't stand to be in the same room with you," he rises with a pained expression and moves to the living room. I hate when he behaves this way. Doesn't he get it? What I really want is for him to hold me and kiss me.

Why don't I say what I mean and mean what I say? That's David's point precisely. But if I told him, "Look, you big lug, I want you to hug me and kiss me even when I'm ranting like a banshee," I would sound inexplicably ludicrous. Shouldn't he already know to do this anyway?

The second worst thing about fighting with David is that I love him. No, I take that back. I adore him. If I did not care about him, about our marriage, the tuna-and-cheese casserole would blister and burn and I would take it out of the oven, and that would be that. It would matter little what was said. There would be nothing to lose. With David, I have plenty on the line. A family, a home, a future. The promises we made to each other. I do not want a life without him, but sometimes . . . sometimes . . .

When we argue, my rumbling, grumbling heart even sounds funny, like a cat being taken to the vet in a box. My skin feels raw. And the hours that follow an argument—oh, my! This emotional aftermath is sister to post-traumatic stress. After a fight the world seems insulting and dull. The most trivial obstacles turn monumental. I bark at the kids. I get sassy with my boss. I either stuff my face with junk or gag at the thought of food. Concentration is difficult, writing impossible. If it is nighttime, I toss and turn in my sleep. I wake with a numbness that begins at my center and ripples through to the ends of my limbs.

I want him to take me in his arms. And rock me, rock me, rock me. But I'm also tempted to give him a good uppercut to the chin.

I've concluded that there are different types of fights, and even the most saintly of couples have engaged in one kind or another. (I've heard that some couples don't fight, but I've never been in that kind of relationship and have never known one, either.) There are fights that resolve the issue at hand and fights that do nothing but help a participant vent. There are fights whose sole purpose is to hurt the other person and fights that repeat a recurring theme. Some fights seem to be about one thing but are really about something else completely. And there are, of course, stupid fights, ones that get started over some minuscule irritation and then take on a life of their own. Silent fights, those that rumble beneath the surface unrecognized, are the most dangerous, I think. Consider an earthquake. Once the friction of opposing plates is too strong to contain, the fissures and cracks and craters it creates are impossible to fix or detain.

Each of us has a particular style of fighting. We are deliberate and calm (David) or hot and cold (me). Some people walk away, some people become highly emotional. Some scream, some clam up. I've also heard it said that we love and fight like our parents did. I wonder about that.

My parents, as of this writing, have been married forty-six years. Their arguments, the ones we witness at least, are more entertaining than a Bill Cosby routine. My mother parries, my father spars. She rolls her eyes, he shrugs his shoulders. Both wave their hands, snicker, snort, pace. They argue in Spanish, but you don't need to know the language to understand. The rise and fall of their voices, the looks, the exaggerated mannerisms, all this gives them away.

Their arguments are a well-rehearsed pas de deux, one step in reply to another, one move mirrored in the next. What do they fight about? The picayune: whether the Florida Marlins should have brought in another pitcher from the bullpen, the number of desserts my father has eaten, why my mother insists on cooking on Mother's Day. After that many years and that many hardships, I imagine there are few new battles to wage and certainly little virgin territory to claim.

Some time ago, I read (probably in one of those how-to articles so ubiquitous in women's magazines) that, like real estate, the three most important factors in fighting fair begin with an L: *Listen, listen, listen.* In the heat of battle, this requires Herculean effort, believe me. Lots of times, I appear to be listening because my mouth is quiet, but I'm really just waiting for my turn, ready to pounce. David always suggests that we repeat, in our own words, what the other has said, to make sure we're actually hearing what is being argued. At first I thought this patently offensive to my intelligence, but it does force me to listen and to understand. Occasionally, it also lowers the temperature on the cheese-and-tuna casserole.

This article I read also stated that conflict was inevitable between couples, but that the way to handle differences constructively could be learned. It listed some commonsense tips: Identify the problem, keep to the subject, resist name-calling, respect the other person, and take responsibility for your actions.

Sounds simple, no? But in the short, triangular distance running from my heart to my head then to my mouth, minefields abound. The best intentions are often short-circuited in terrible and embarrassing ways. Even if I begin a fight calmly, I rarely end it that way. And honestly, it feels so strange to sit in front of a man who shares your bed and tell him in your office voice, "I get angry when you watch TV all night and don't talk to me. It makes me feel like I don't matter to you." That doesn't adequately portray the depth of hurt and disappointment. It seems so . . . so sanitized.

If fighting fair is an art, I'm a mere apprentice. Then again, I doubt anyone truly masters the form. Each sculpture, each watercolor, each manuscript, each argument, produces an invaluable lesson. String those lessons together and a couple might be able to come up with rules that pertain to their particular situation. David and I know, for instance, that arguments and evenings are a volatile mixture. Fighting at night when we're tired and cranky invariably turns disastrous. We know, too, that certain words set off the fire alarm in our hearts. We try not to shout them. We avoid ultimatums.

Most of the time.

Truth is, he is better at this than I am. Truth is, my efforts are sporadic. Sometimes, the anger has festered so long that I don't want to follow rules, any rules. Sometimes, something he has done or said or failed to do seems so infuriatingly insensitive that I lose all sense of perspective.

For some couples, fighting is a way of life. That's all they do, and that's what they are good at. A friend of mine tells me stories about his first marriage that make it sound like a war zone. A nightly argument was as predictable as the dinner salad. Anything would set her off—if he was a few minutes late from work, if he had forgotten the dry cleaners, if she figured he wasn't helping around the house, if he spoke to another woman. From day to day, he never knew what the argument du jour would be, only that it was certain. He concluded that she *enjoyed* fighting, liked the fireworks and the confrontations. After a while, it became their only form of communication, the ultimate connection in their marriage. I don't call this a marriage, though. I think of it as hell without the trimmings.

Lovers' spats are perversely intriguing, especially if they are public. I've read about a doozy or two. About Madonna, Sean Penn, Mariah Carey, Pamela Lee Anderson. Et cetera. Et cetera. Et cetera. I'm not quite sure why we're so interested, except that it's a little like rubbernecking after a traffic accident. Publicly we say, *Those idiots!* But in the privacy of our hearts, we mutter: *There but for the grace of God go I.*

There's an old saying in Spanish that comes to mind when I think about fights and their logical (and hopeful) conclusion. *Las doñas y las palomas, aunque salgan con gemidos, tornan a sus nidos.* Translated literally, it means: Women, like pigeons, may complain, but they always return to their nests. In other words, making up is inevitable.

Like arguments, reconciliations often follow a pattern. Some are slow, others sudden. Many begin with a gesture or a word, a few with a well-placed note. Truces tend to be uneasy, but most, if not all, conclude with lovemaking, sessions that are particularly, wonderfully tender. I think this is because of the realization of what could have been lost and what should be forgiven. Forgiveness is a strange thing among lovers, though. It's verbally granted before it's wholeheartedly given, and the promise of it is as much carrot as stick.

Still, the ability to apologize and the need to forgive are essential to a relationship. So is humor. In fact, there's nothing like a good laugh in the middle of a tense fight to help clear the passages of understanding. If there is anything David and I do well in our arguments, surely it must be finding humor in the middle of the shouting. Sometimes we can't even help ourselves. Humor creeps in unexpectedly.

During our last argument, I mistook something David was saying. I heard him say "small tomatoes" instead of "stupid ultimatums." Now, I know that confusing the two may beg suspension of disbelief, but I wasn't wearing contact lenses or glasses during this fight and when I can't see, I don't hear well either. In any case, as soon as he said "small tomatoes/stupid ultimatums," I stood and threw up my hands in surrender.

"What," I asked, "do small tomatoes have to do with anything?"

So, David, here's your small tomatoes essay.

Through the Valley of the Shadow of Death

⁓⁓

She had locked herself inside the bathroom by mistake. I could hear her fiddling with the handle, then rattling the door.

Exasperated, I walked down the hall and tried opening it myself. Nothing.

"Mabel," I called out, "are you okay?"

"*Sí, sí,*" she replied, though the undercurrent of fear in her voice implied something else.

"Don't panic. Just listen to me and I'll tell you how to open the door."

Silence.

"You there?"

"Uh-huh."

"Listen to me, okay? I want you to do as I tell you. If you get confused or don't understand, tell me right away."

She agreed. I dictated the instructions carefully and slowly: Find the lever in the center of the lock. Twist it until it's horizontal.

"Horizontal?" Mabel didn't understand what that meant. I had to simplify.

More instructions: Turn the lever until it's lying down, from side to side. Then slide the door to your left.

There was a scratching on the door, a click. I tried sliding the door myself, but no luck.

"Look," I told her, "all I want you to do is unlock the door. Move the lever so it's sideways instead of up and down. Do you understand?"

She didn't say anything for several seconds, but there was the sound of movement, a solid step and a swooshing, then the flush of the toilet.

"Are you okay, Mabel?"

"It's all over the floor."

"What's all over the floor?" *Dear Lord,* I thought, *she clogged the damn toilet, and on a Sunday, too. Jesus, Jesus!*

She began to cry.

"Why. Are. You. Crying. Now?" I couldn't keep the anger out of my voice.

"I can't get out."

"Yes, you can. Just follow my instructions. Do what I tell you."

After a couple more tries with what I considered to be simple but explicit explanations, Mabel had not opened the lock and I had lost the little patience I had left. An unpleasant smell was wafting my way. Frustrated, I banged on the door with my fist. "Don't move from there," I ordered.

Like she was going anywhere.

I returned with my daughter, a bread knife, a metal hanger, and a paper clip.

"Is that you?" Mabel called.

"Who else?" I groused.

Within minutes, the lock clicked open. I pushed the door.

"Oh shit! Oh shit! Oh shit!" I whispered in disbelief.

My daughter jumped back. "Gross!" she shrieked.

There was shit everywhere, on the toilet seat, all over the floor, up the walls, and behind the counter, shit spread like lava over a valley. Mabel had it on her hands and her robe and her shoes, and she stood before us with her eyes wide open and her face streaked with tears, a ribbon of toilet paper stuck to her side. The smell was putrid. I gagged. My daughter ran to another bathroom, holding her hands over her face.

"I tried to . . ." Mabel began.

"I know," I said. "I know."

Armed with enough equipment to vanquish a plague, my daughter and I washed Mabel from head to toe, then bundled up her clothes and slippers in a plastic trash bag. We dressed her and put her to bed. We hardly spoke while working, stopping every so often to wince or step away for fresh air. The cleanup of the bathroom itself took us an entire afternoon, but the horrible smell lingered for a long while after, despite a good scrubbing with bleach and other disinfectants.

That day, I decided to put my mother-in-law in a boarding home for older adults.

Mabel Suarez was diagnosed with Alzheimer's disease three days before Christmas. She was sixty-seven years old. Less than two weeks later, her only child, my husband Leo, died of a massive heart attack at thirty-seven. I inherited his mother.

That line, at first, was a joke. Over time, the situation grew less funny and more burdensome. Over time, too, I wavered between resentment and guilt, anger and embarrassment. I couldn't quite figure out how I had ended up caring for someone who was not my flesh and blood, someone who, in the best of circumstances, would not have made my list of favorite people. Her older sister, herself burdened by an elderly husband, helped tremendously, but the bulk of the decisions—the buying of diapers, the delivery of food supplements, the questions for the doctor—inevitably fell to me. This decision making, quite frankly, was worse than cleaning up feces, because I did not know when it would end or if it would accomplish anything. Alzheimer's is a surreptitious thief, a killer who arrives benignly but leaves broken lives, lost memories, and dashed hopes in its wake.

Mabel had never been a woman of much independence, so when she began exhibiting early signs of the disease, both her son and I chalked it up to old age. She wanted more attention, we thought.

She was scared of being alone, we said. But when she went on a rare trip to Spain that summer, her sister returned with stories that were too troubling to ignore. Mabel couldn't pay for her purchases. She would often forget where she was. And she lost her train of thought in mid-sentence. That, we suspected, was more than simple aging.

When confronted with these telling details, however, Mabel insisted that unfamiliar surroundings and the anxiety of being away from home had confused her. We, in turn, wanted so much to believe this was true—she rarely left home to do anything on her own—that neither Leo nor I thought about it again. So many more pressing responsibilities called. A new baby. Rebuilding a home after Hurricane Andrew. Stressful jobs. Children's schoolwork and baseball games.

Her memory loss and her inability to perform some very basic daily tasks did not go away, though. They only worsened. A trusted handyman called to tell us that she had written him a check for two thousand and some dollars instead of two hundred. Worse, she didn't know how to correct it. Soon after, she began to accuse her son of stealing from her. Money, she told relatives, kept disappearing every time he visited her. She phoned me one day and asked me if he had a gambling problem (he didn't) or a drug problem (not that either). Later, she could not remember this conversation.

Finally, we decided to seek medical help. Leo made an appointment at a memory-disorder clinic, but when it came time to take her, I ended up doing the honors. We argued about that, of course. I wanted him to take time off from work; he swore it was impossible that week. He volunteered to reschedule; I insisted we couldn't wait any longer, even if it meant rescheduling my own workday.

During the twenty-minute drive to her home, I grumbled and muttered and complained: *Stuck with her again.* I pulled up her driveway. She was sitting in a lawn chair on her tiled porch, a brown purse at her feet.

"You're so good to me," she greeted me.

Read this and you might think of me as an exemplary daughter-in-law. I don't know if I deserve that praise. The resentment of being "stuck again" was always there, tempered by a sense of duty and eventually by affection. When her son was alive, there was an obvious connection between the two of us. We both loved the same man, in different ways but with similar passion, and that love served as both bond and anchor. When he died, I discovered that the two of us had developed something more, too. I couldn't always define it, but in the four years, one month, and one day that I considered myself responsible for her, it became the star by which I set my course.

Relationships with in-laws are fragile arrangements. They become relatives by virtue of a commitment to another person. Move away in some fashion—divorce, for example—and there's no longer a claim. The relationship evaporates. If a connection remains, it usually involves children, a mutual purpose of raising them.

In-laws, mothers in particular, can be (and often are) a source of problems and arguments for many couples. Mabel did not fit the mold. She was not the meddling mother-in-law of popular lore and, far from selfish, she was always willing to help out. I did not feel comfortable allowing her to do so, however. She became too flustered in emergencies, and the children ran circles around her. (One time, when she baby-sat the three oldest grandkids, they locked her out of the house. Another time, they tied her to a chair with a belt.) But I wonder now if my reluctant acceptance of her offers said less about her abilities and more about me and how I regarded any intrusion into my married life. I had grown up in a household with a grandmother who was everything one abhors in an in-law—and more. She interfered, intruded, manipulated, and my mother paid the price for more than forty years. I was not willing to follow in my mother's footsteps, and I informed Leo about that soon after we were engaged. It proved to be a moot pronouncement. Mabel liked living in her own house.

My mother-in-law had been a teacher in a small town in Cuba. In black-and-white photos of her posing with her classes, she had a round face and serious eyes. It seems she did not smile easily. Exiled in the United States, she never worked as a teacher again, but was employed in several jobs before settling (until her early retirement) as a keypunch operator for a national retail chain of upscale stores. I always thought this to be a good thing because I found it impossible to imagine this small, timid woman in charge of a classroom of American hellions.

Mabel was scared of life, fearful of trying anything new and of performing the most elementary tasks alone. For this, I never forgave her. In some ways, she was typical of women in her culture and of her time, raised to be married and to live the rest of their lives relying on their husbands, then on their children. She never learned to drive. She didn't cook. My father-in-law did the bulk of the grocery shopping and most, if not all, of the decision making. All holidays were spent at her son's house, our house, or tagging along with my side of the family.

Though she was ecstatic with the arrival of her first grandchild, she did not carry him for weeks because she was afraid of dropping him or having him roll off her lap. She sat beside his crib all night to make sure the baby would not choke. At a church fair once, as one of her grandchildren rode on a flying-elephant ride, she collapsed in fear, wailing and hyperventilating. She saw danger everywhere. Her fears affected her physically, too. A hypochondriac, she reveled in the most minor ailments. If she heard of an illness or read about a disease, within days she began complaining about similar symptoms. She visited her doctor weekly, and we never knew the difference between the very real aches and pains of aging and the imagined troubles of her own making.

"My mother," my late husband complained, "is the only person I know who likes being sick."

But being sick had its purpose, I think. It was a way of getting attention from a son who was busy with his own family and a husband who went from ignoring her completely to belittling her in front of people. Yet, Mabel could—and did—surprise me. Before Alzheimer's, she cared for her bedridden elderly mother for several years, keeping a schedule of bathing, feeding, and medicating that was as precise and detailed as D day. And she did this while working. Not long after her mother's death, her husband suffered a stroke, and the last year of their lives together was surely a trial for her. He was the worst sort of patient, insulting, capricious, and demanding. She endured in spite of this. Later, she was called upon once again to take care of another dying man, a young second cousin whom she had helped raise. All in all, she was the family's nursemaid for five years, unpaid and hardly appreciated. It seemed incredibly sad to me that when it was her turn to be cared for, none of us was there to do it as selflessly as she had done for others. It was also incredibly ironic that when her Alzheimer's worsened and other illnesses cropped up—pneumonia, infections, acute anemia—she could not savor this final sickness.

After her son died, Mabel initially remained in the coral-colored duplex where she had lived most of her life in Miami. Her sister visited often and I when I could. She kept her house spotless. Sometimes, she worked in her garden in the backyard, but she began forgetting what needed watering and replanting and trimming. So she ignored the plants except when I came over. Then, together we would survey the yard. If any of the plants were in a difficult spot to water—hanging ferns beyond her reach, mainly—she would ask for my help. "You're so good to me," she would say, as I sprayed the leaves. It seemed that every time I poured water over the corn plants or the philodendron or the potted palm, we connected in some simple way. Despite my reluctance, I began to take an interest in her plants.

Because she had never liked to cook, she subsisted on very little and lost weight quickly. On Thursday afternoons, I would pick her up on my way from work, then deliver her home Monday or Tuesday morning, depending on my schedule. She was always waiting for me, in the porch's lawn chair before the weather turned brutal, or in her living room with the front door open when it was summer. Always, too, she said something nice to me. You look good in that color. Or, I like how you are wearing your hair. Or, You've gained a little weight. (That, among Cubans, is a compliment.) She was, yes, trying to ingratiate herself with me, but there was something else going on, too. In hindsight, I realize she wanted my accept-ance, that pat on the back or nod of approval that would validate her in some way. She just wasn't sure how to go about it.

After a neighbor found her wandering several blocks from home one Tuesday night, her sister and I agreed she needed a paid com-panion to watch over her. We were worried, too, that she wasn't eating properly. We hired a nice woman with a lot of energy, but that arrangement didn't last long: The woman left one Monday morning and never returned. Mabel began spending more time at my house, full weekends slipping into mid-week, then Monday through Sunday through Monday again, until I decided she might as well move in. The children were delighted, especially the two younger ones. She was content playing with them for hours, watch-ing them roughhouse in the backyard, and never reprimanding them. They played board games on the dining-room table, games she could no longer figure out, and soldiers on the floor of the kids' bedroom.

It was not always an idyllic existence, however. The memory loss was precipitous and increasingly noticeable. Her grooming turned sloppy. Sometimes, she wouldn't comb her hair or brush her teeth, yet she always carried a little purse full of old makeup. Dressing be-came a challenge. She couldn't figure out how to put on her shoes or blouse; sleeves proved to be an obstacle course. At the kitchen table, she stared at the food and utensils without a clue to what they were for. A few times, she walked into the garage or the utility room when she intended to stroll to the backyard. She forgot the chil-dren's names and repeatedly asked for me even when I was stand-ing right in front of her.

The deterioration was sad, but at times it was also funny. Or we thought so. Maybe we just needed to laugh. One night at the din-ner table, unsure of what to do with her glass of milk, she poured it over her meat. The little ones thought this hilarious and begged to do the same. Occasionally, she mismatched her socks or wore some item of clothing on her head. That, too, elicited a round of chuckles, but as these actions became more commonplace, the laughter gave way to concern, then frustration, and finally anger.

I had had the best of intentions (I think)—and so had the children—when we first moved her in with us, but it became difficult to lead a "normal" life. Fearful of what she might do, we could not leave her alone on weekends, which meant she was carted off to places that made her confusion worse. At a Mass following a retreat my oldest son had attended, she insisted on walking up and down the rows of people during the homily. She became loud and began to weep. At home, she hallucinated. The children were trying to steal her money, she complained. We were having drunken orgies at night. We were starving her. We were trying to drive her crazy by playing music too loud.

For the children, she was no longer fun. For me . . . for me . . .

The first adult-living facility Mabel stayed at was not far from where we lived. It was a single-family residence where the owner and the employees spoke Spanish and cooked Cuban fare. That had been very important to me in the search for a home because I wanted stability and familiarity for her. That wasn't enough, though. The first day I left her, her screaming curses followed me to the car. I drove home so shaken I got very little work done that day. It wasn't any different the first times I visited her either, and when I took the children to see her, she grabbed them and told them she was being held prisoner so I could take her money. Their dead father, she threatened, would rise from his grave to punish our transgression. Frightened by this reaction, her sister talked about moving Mabel into the second room of her apartment. No, no, no, I insisted, she's in the best place she could be.

About a year later, that boarding home closed, and I rushed around to find another one. Within weeks, I realized the second facility was a mistake. The care was dismal, the attitude worse. I had expected the mental deterioration, but was alarmed at the ground she was losing physically. Two days after I discovered her face bruised from a fall, I moved her to a third home, then weeks later to a fourth. By this time, she was in diapers and in a wheelchair. She neither recognized me nor called for me by name. The once plump woman was skin and bones.

The children refused to visit their grandmother. "I don't want to remember her like that," one of my sons said. I continued to go, usually once or twice a week, hurried stopovers wedged between orthodontist appointments, baseball practices, and work deadlines. My visits were predictable. I arrived with something for her to eat, sweet Maria crackers, or pound cake, or powdered doughnuts. I fed her in small portions so she wouldn't choke. I asked her questions. She answered them in incoherent sentences. I checked on her medication, doctors' visits, the various aches and pains she had complained about the previous week. Sometimes I arrived bearing bags of Ensure, the food supplement, and Depends diapers. Occasionally, I left with new prescriptions. By then, I had become the point guard for her supplemental insurance, her pension, her Medicare, posing as her daughter to expedite transactions. By then, too, she had forgotten how to curse.

On October 9, five days after I remarried, Mabel was rushed to the hospital with a blood infection. Doctors said she had two or three days to live, five at the most, so her sister quickly made funeral arrangements. I did not know any of this until I returned home. From the airport, my husband drove me north to the hospital. A Sunday night, the corridors were empty and the smell of alcohol and illness strong. She lay tethered to beeping machines, a withered mass of skin and graying hair adrift in a sea of white.

"Mabel, Mabel, Mabel," I called to her.

She did not move. She didn't even twitch.

For the first couple of weeks, her sister visited her daily, trying to coax her back to some semblance of life. Doctors pumped all kinds of antibiotics into her veins. So, in spite of dire medical predictions, Mabel's condition improved enough to warrant her transfer to another hospital. This improvement, though, was minor. Truth was, Mabel was kept alive unnecessarily because of medical zealousness, technological miracles, and my own ignorance. Time and time again, I approved tests and transfusions that kept her condition stable but did nothing for her quality of life.

Finally, more than three months after she had entered the hospital, I asked the social worker for information about hospice. I was exhausted from so many decisions; she had been pricked and picked, sliced and spliced so many times that no good vein remained for an IV. After some research, she was moved to a nursing home with clear instructions for no resuscitation or other life-prolonging procedures.

Then, in the waning hours of a February night, the phone rang at home. This was not uncommon, for nurses at the hospital had often called at unusual hours to get my verbal approval for some emergency medical procedure.

"Your mother," the solemn voice said on the other end, "is not doing well. You might want to come see her."

I stumbled out of the house, into my car, then through the halls of the nursing home to Mabel's room. I sat in a chair beside Mabel and took her hand. She felt feverish, and her breath came in short gasps punctuated by infuriatingly long pauses.

"Mabel. Mabel."

Her eyes fluttered open once, twice, then remained closed. A nurse came in to take her pulse, then left. I sat next to her, holding her hand, for I don't know how long. The darkness of night seemed to deepen. I may have fallen asleep sitting up.

The nurse returned, took her pulse again. The expression on her face confirmed my suspicions. "Are there any other family members you want to call?" she asked softly.

I phoned her sister, who lived about two hours away. I phoned home and asked my husband to wake up the two older boys. I wanted them to say goodbye. When I hung up, the nurse patted my back.

"Talk to her now. Tell her it's all right for her to go," she instructed before leaving.

I picked up a card on the night table and began to read Psalm 23 in Spanish. At the end, the words caught in my throat. I looked down at Mabel, at the face lined with the last attempts at life, at her dry, gasping mouth, at the sunken sockets of her eyes. A tear punctured the blanket, then another and another and another. I whispered the psalm again, a comforting song.

The boys arrived, hands in their pockets and eyes bleary from sleep. They waited at the threshold as though embarrassed to come in. I told them to say goodbye to their grandmother. But when they approached the bed, they hesitated and turned back to me. Who was this gaunt, gasping figure curled in a fetal position over too many pillows?

There were tears in their voices when they talked, and confusion, too. They kissed her and stood awkwardly side by side, two teenagers who were quickly becoming much too familiar with the inevitability of death. As they left, I asked them to help their stepfather with the younger children.

I've heard it said that when someone dies, all those loved ones who have gone before return to help ease the way. If that is true, then her son, my first husband, hovered somewhere about the room that night. I wish I could say I felt him, but I really never did. I felt instead something at the pit of my stomach, not pain, but a dull ache, like the onset of nausea.

"*Ya te puedes ir, Mabel,*" I whispered. "*Descansa.*" You can go now. Rest.

As dawn's first light seeped past the windowsill of her room, her fingertips began to grow cold, the pause between breaths longer.

"*Descansa, Mabel,*" I repeated. "*Descansa.*"

Her breath became shallow, shallower. I stood to kiss her forehead, then felt the pulse at the side of her neck, so faint. I sat down again and pressed my face against her hand.

The Lord is my Shepherd, I shall not want.
He maketh me lie down in green pastures;
He leadeth me beside the still waters.
He restoreth my soul;

He leadeth me in the paths of righteousness for His name's
  sake.
Yea, though I walk through the valley of the shadow of death,
  I will fear no evil . . .

I felt relieved when she stopped breathing. Oh, such relief! Is
that wrong? Was I selfish?

At unusual times—when there's a sale for her food supplement,
say, or when I spot her favorite doughnuts in the grocery aisle—I
think of Mabel and of the twenty-three years I knew her, and
judged her. Her possessions distributed, she remains with us in that
certain way memory becomes presence. Her life and slow descent
into the abyss of Alzheimer's served as an object lesson for me.
Much of my caregiving, I now know, had little to do with her needs
and plenty to do with mine. Like her, I wanted validation, proof
that by performing these selfless acts I was good and kind and deserving of a life her own son had lost. I also wanted forgiveness of
some kind, absolution from the harsh words and thoughtless acts
of my married life I had come to regret. She was a connection to my
late husband, and I yearned, desperately, painfully, for that.
  Did I understand all this when I began caring for her? Of course
not. Not for a long time.
  When she was alive, she longed for a special relationship with
me, for moments of shared intimacy and traded confessions. Her
sister used to tell me that Mabel had secretly pined for a daughter
and figured that the woman her son married might turn out to be
like a daughter for her. I never was, and I didn't want to be. Yet, a
kind of intimacy did develop after her son died and her illness
worsened. There were no shopping trips together or heart-baring
conversations in the kitchen, none of the traditional trappings of female friendships. But intimacy comes in many shapes, sometimes in
the black grains of potted soil, sometimes in a shared interest in
ferns and impatiens. I think now of all the times I checked her
plants for mealy bugs, all the times I trimmed the yellowing leaves

and mixed plant food in her blue bucket, and I realize that not all close associations need words and explanations. Actions are plenty. One doesn't water a garden without eventually caring for its blooms—or its weeds.

Biscayne Bay

We leave the Miami Beach boat ramp as the sky turns the color of pewter and northern Biscayne Bay waters darken to meet the inexorable march of dusk. Already, that feeling of done day has settled into the air. Our guide for the night is Bob LeMay, a round-faced, mustached captain who wears flip-flops and earth-color shorts and polo shirts to work. He maneuvers his seventeen-foot, baby-blue Maverick north, northwest, between the mainland's high-rises and highways on one side and the line of mansions and hotels on the other. A porpoise jumps once, twice, then disappears. A heron flies back from her job. In the waning light, we can still make out the contrasts in bay bottom, grassy shallows dropping off to the clearer gray-blue of deeper water.

Bob kills the engine at a rock flat north of Mount Sinai Hospital and fires off instructions. In search of trout, David will use a popper fly. From the bow, he casts, the orange line a thin ray of escaped sunlight as it soars across. The fly, white and feathery, lands and floats on the bay. David strips. Plop!zzz!Plop!zzz! goes the fly. Nothing bites. He casts again, strips, reels. The water ripples. He does this several times without any luck.

We drift east and south. To our left, the sun finally slides behind the glass buildings, re-painting the sky in pastels of cotton candy and sherbet. Darkness descends. Lights blink on, inverted stars against the black of early evening. On the water, I can no longer tell the difference between the flats and the deep; the texture of the bay is that smooth, like suede. The air smells wet, and the wind has cooled.

As David casts, Bob baits my hook with a bright yellow jig. He shows me how to work the jig to get the right action to attract fish. I cast from the stern, a jerky movement that sends the yellow plastic soaring embarrassingly high into the air instead of in a graceful arch, more pop fly than line drive. Neither of the men says anything, but I know what they're thinking. Trying to overcome my inadequacy, I reel in with swift, smooth movements, hoping my imitation of live bait will attract a bite. The fish are not impressed. I cast, reel. Cast, reel. Cast, reel. Nothing.

In search of better luck, we move to another spot. Hopeful, David and I cast again, he on one end of the boat, I on the other. Except for another small vessel that pulls away minutes after we begin to fish, we seem to have the bay all to ourselves. The solitude is wonderfully refreshing. But the fish ignore our attempts. They're either not hungry or they're onto us.

Undaunted, we motor to more fertile waters, this time to the waterfront backyard of a million-dollar home where dock floodlights cast the kinds of large, protective shadows that tarpon, a silvery game fish of the warmer Atlantic, seek. And, whoa! there they are, long, graceful animals flitting from light to dark, seemingly unaware of our intrusion. They're three, four feet, large, but Bob and David assure me these are mere babies, only ten to forty pounds. David is so excited he bounds for the bow and stumbles over one of his shoes. This does little to slow him down, though. Unbalanced, he still manages to cast. The tarpon spot the fly and swim toward it. We hold our breath. They swim closer, closer, circle it—but then pass right by it, uninterested. We exhale noisily.

I cast, allow the jig to settle. I work the jig toward me, slowly, patiently. A tarpon follows. He opens his mouth—and SUCKS the jig in!

"Set the hook!" Bob shouts.

I yank the rod up. The tarpon runs, jumps once. Snap! It's gone. I reel in the broken line. Bob pats me on the back.

"Way to go," says David. "Your first one."

For a few more minutes, I watch the ease of the fish as they swim and the quick, expert motions of David's hand as he slides the fly across the water. I listen to Bob's whispered instructions. I'm still living the excitement of the brief moment with my fugitive tarpon. I can almost taste the tension, a metallic flavor not unlike blood. It occurs to me that I—all of us, animal and man, sea and sky—are starring in a special, one-evening engagement, a play whose central theme is the art of pretense. Fishing is about that, about pretense and deceit. It's about a fly or a jig assuming the role of live fish and about fish trying to get away with a free lunch. Yet, everything in this act on the bay—the tarpon swimming, David casting, Bob instructing—appears to be mere background for the real drama. I sense a hidden plot line.

Bob confirms this when we abandon the mansion's dock and aim south for the metal-and-concrete spans that connect Miami to Miami Beach. The tide is falling now, and the underworld of Biscayne Bay is coming alive to conform to the ages-old tidal cycle. As the current moves out, it carries with it finger mullet, shrimp, and whitebait. This movement attracts predators, who wait in the shadows of bridges as unaware prey, each no bigger than a thumb, slip by.

We want front-row seats for this ambush, so Bob drives us through the center span of a bridge, then back to a spot downcurrent where the tarpon are hunting between the lights and the shadowline of the bridge. He turns off the engine and sidles up to the barnacle-encrusted pilings.

"Okay, fishies," he calls out. "Here we are. Where are you?"

To underscore Bob's words, David casts into the edge of a shadow. One second, two seconds, three, four . . . Bingo! All hell breaks loose. Bob pushes us off the bridge pilings, turns on the engine, and maneuvers us out into open water. In the middle of the fight, the tarpon jumps, a silver creature gloriously shiny in the night. It runs. David reels. He yanks, he gives. The fight appears to be a draw. Suddenly, the line breaks. David groans. The best ones always seem to get away.

We head back to the shadowline. Worried about my lack of expertise, Bob blind casts for me, then turns over my spinning rod. Almost instantly, I feel a tug and instinctively jerk up: I'm ready for this one. Then everything happens so fast. Bob motors us out from under the bridge. David is shouting instructions I don't understand. The fish is trying to run away. I pull and reel. I sweep sideways and use my weight. (*This is a baby tarpon?* I think. *Haha!*) I bow as it jumps. I tug this way, that. My arms shake. After several minutes of this struggle, Bob concludes that the tarpon, which usually would head upcurrent away from the bridge, has instead doubled back on itself and sought refuge around the pilings. It has decided to wait me out. We motor in under the bridge to go after it. Again, I tug and bow and pull and reel—but all for naught. It eventually shreds my leader against the pilings.

"That's why they call it fishing, not catching," David consoles me.

Later that night, I jump six tarpon and catch one, bringing it so close to the boat that Bob grabs the leader and releases the fish. David, too, jumps six and boats one. His is magnificent, large-mouthed and sleek, its color a cross between chrome and blue. I snap the obligatory photos and we release the fish into the bay. Tarpon is nonedible, and David believes in letting go of his catch.

Nearing one a.m., almost four and a half hours after we launched, we chug back to the ramp, ecstatic and high on adrenaline. I realize that we have neither eaten dinner nor had any water to drink during our fishing trip. Suddenly I'm thirsty and famished. A few yards from the boat docks, revelers in skin-tight clothing and moussed hair walk to one of the nearby clubs that has made South Beach a hot-hot nightspot. Their perfume assaults the air. They do not even notice the other kind of nightlife so close to them, that one lurking beneath the surface, a teeming, heaving existence secreted in these waters. And they surely cannot imagine the wild music I have just danced to. Just as well. I don't want too many people to know about it. Sometimes to love a place (or a person), you must say nothing about it.

As we walk back to the car, I turn to look at the glittering expanse of black beyond the dock and under the bridges. Miami is a city of watery beauty, of moonlight and streetlight shimmering off bay and ocean, lakes and rivers. Water is everywhere we turn, to the west from the swampy Everglades, to the south on the stepping-stones of the Florida Keys, to the east in ripples of ocean. For me, Biscayne Bay is the most enchanting of these, the most approachable. I know the bay best during the day, when its magic is plain in the brazen light of noon. I know it with the roar of motorboats and the flash of sailboat colors. But at night, it is no less precious and bewitching. Either way, day or night, the bay's beauty is dignified, unsullied, so unlike some of the garishness we've built on land.

To look at Biscayne Bay is to marvel at the many hues of blue that nature can draw from its private palette. The clear blue of shallows or the murky blue of mudbottom. The blue-green tinged by seagrass. The lapis lazuli of distant waters. The stiff blue of horizon line. The indigo ink of deep bay. The turquoise of shores. Then, of course, the aquamarine of changing sea just before rain threatens. Regardless of shade, lighter here, darker there, the blue appears unending. Vast. Ambitious. Intransigent.

The bay is a shallow marine lagoon, warm and inviting, about thirty-five miles long, from Haulover Inlet to the Midnight Pass, and varying from one mile to eight in width. I love it best under a light chop, when sun diamonds sparkle just so off the surface and the foam of a cresting wave smudges the immensity of blue with a dot of white. It is a liquid window to a world that existed long before I arrived, before anybody came, and which, if we are careful and conscientious, will continue long after we are gone. Thousands of years in the making, the bay is a series of paradoxes. It is vibrant where it is most old, wild during a stormy afternoon, peaceful the next morning. Its very strangeness becomes familiar. Like the rings in the trunk of an old oak tree, the nuances of the bay's moods are what make it, in part, so appealing.

In 1513, Spanish explorer Ponce de Leon sailed across this bay in search of the Fountain of Youth. Like most of us, he was looking for a good idea in the wrong place—or better said, he was in the right place for all the wrong reasons. He discovered a chain of rocky islets that he christened Los Mártires (The Martyrs) and later named an island south of a sand bar Santa Pola. No one knows the identity of that island and hardly anybody really cares, but I consider the first Spanish name for these lush landmarks incredibly inappropriate—The Martyrs, for heaven's sake! In spite of his strong spirit of adventure, Ponce de Leon suffered from a most human fault: the inability to recognize serendipity.

Without reading journals of his travels, I know exactly what Ponce de Leon saw, or more precisely what he failed to see: mangrove-rimmed shores, brown pelicans and white ibis, snowy egrets and blue heron, transparent waters stroked with seagrass, and fish of many colors. These are the things I point out to my children when we drift across mudflats or motor down a channel. I am trying to teach them to see, and when they see to notice, and when they notice to appreciate. I do not want them to pursue the Fountain of Youth or some other mythical hope when something better thrives right in their own backyard.

The first act of appreciation is to notice the mangroves and the tangled web their timber weaves. The roots of the red mangroves grow down from branches overhead or arch like stiff, arthritic legs into the water. Here, lapping insolently to its own beat, the water is brackish, stained brown by the tannins of the trees. For years, mangroves were thought of as a nuisance, as freaks of nature. But the almost impenetrable forest they form serves as both buffer and filter, preventing soil from washing into the bay while also serving as a wall against the wind and waves of hurricanes. Mangroves' fallen leaves feed bacteria and other tiny organisms, which, in turn, serve as food for the bigger marine animals. I often think of them as a haven for mosquitoes on a steady diet of steroids. To get close to a mangrove coastline is to risk an infestation of bites. Yet, more than sucking, hovering insects live along this snarl of wet wood. Below the surface, you can find the scoot and scurry of small lives. This is where the young come to give birth and where the old come to rest. Snook, snapper, grunt, barracuda, permit, bonefish—they all like the very shadows we so resolutely avoid.

Beyond the mangroves, travel inland to the islands built by billions of tiny coral animals one hundred thousand years ago. Look closely and you'll see fossil rock as hard as an enemy's heart. But on this thin soil just beyond the shores, a tropical forest flourishes, hardwood hammocks of gumbo limbo, Jamaican dogwood, Torchwood, mahogany, and Strangler fig. This mass of crooked trees and intertwined limbs offers a gracious canopy of shade for spiders and birds and rats and raccoons. A Zebra butterfly. A rare Schaus swallowtail. And mosquitoes, too, of course. Always mosquitoes.

Offshore, another treasure. In skinny water grow the marine grasses, waving patches of sea bottom that, from a distance, appear to be dirty water. How strange it feels to walk on a patch or to swim through it; the long green and brown blades are so slippery and slimy, so *prehistoric*. Yuk! Yuk! the children cry out when we paddle through a mound. Yum! Yum! the fish gurgle. The grasses are the kitchens of the sea—dining room, too, if you think in formal terms. This is where all fins come to eat. Yet, to the untrained eye, seagrass is a blotch, an inconvenience that can tangle fishing lines and boat blades. Every once in a while, a propeller or a grounded hull mows a swath of grass so bare that it scars the bottom in a straight, ugly line. It pains me to see such willful, careless desecration of something that doesn't belong to us.

We are a people of the sea, my family. For generations we have lived by it, near it, facing it—the Mediterranean, the Caribbean, the Atlantic. My paternal grandmother spent her childhood in a shoebox-size apartment in Barcelona, within walking distance of the port where Columbus returned from his voyage to the New World to meet with the Spanish sovereigns in the Royal Palace.

Just south of there, in a fishing village now turned posh resort, my mother was born to a champion swimmer who competed in meets along the bay. He once tried to swim the Strait of Gibraltar but failed—and lost his swim trunks along the way. Farther down the coastline, in another tiny town, you can stand on the roof of my paternal grandfather's house and marvel at the turquoise of the Mediterranean, until it bumps hard against the sky, a precipice to the unknown. Somehow, this vista encourages contemplation and daring. It is, depending on your personality, a standing invitation to wander, to search for what's just beyond the horizon. Eventually, that was what my ancestors did. They abandoned this view for another stretch of sea and sky, for the tropical latitudes and warm waters of Cuba.

I think of them sometimes when we run around the bay, a people weathered by the sting of salt water and the blaze of sun and the sweetness of hope. I think how their daring was really desperation, their faith a form of blindness. Departure from land, after all, is always a surrender. It is also a homecoming.

"All of us," David likes to say, "come from the sea."

And so, without gills or webbing, we return to it. We build houses on its edge, explore its fathoms, raid its nurseries, venture forth on its waves. We fashion fins from rubber, water eyes from plastic. Yet, its depths remain a mystery. We know only enough about it to understand that its unexpected fury is a danger past imagining.

I write this as a monster hurricane, the length of the peninsula of Florida and as powerful as another storm that walloped my home years ago, menaces the coast. The possibility of a storm surge has forced the evacuation of hundreds of thousands of people from beaches and other low-lying areas. Just a bit farther inland, we have prepared for the hurricane in our own way—secured the patio furniture, installed the shutters, hoarded enough canned goods to last us through apocalypse. But in the cavelike darkness of our house, we know there is only so much protection when the weather turns, when the ocean rises.

"You can hide from the wind," warns a forecaster from the National Hurricane Center, "but you can't hide from the water."

The film clip of his prediction is played on the television again and again for days. It makes me remember something I have not thought about in years, one of my mother's favorite sayings: *Guárdate del agua mansa que de la recia te guarda Dios.* Beware of tame waters for God will protect you from the chop. Did somebody think of this while staring out at the deceptive stillness of a bay?

It is a morning of silver beginnings, lush clouds against an opulent sky. The pelicans are barely awake on the channel markers when we pass them, bills flattened against feathery bellies, wings flush against brown sides. A willet soars by, its black-and-white wing-stripe a flash of contrast over the deep green of mangrove leaves. A lone stork wades near the roots, sweeping its bill through the water. To the right of us, due south, loom the towers of the Turkey Point Power Plant, and to the left, the hazy silhouette of a landfill that locals call Mount Trashmore. Straight ahead: Elliott Key, a sliver of land with transparent shores. This is where, in waist-high waters as still as a bowl of broth, we usually anchor for lunch. It is too early to eat, though, so we head north to the flats along Sands Key. Off the curving southern lip of the island, David cuts the engine, climbs onto the platform of the skiff, and begins to pole us across shallow waters. Bail open, hook baited, I help him search for prey. We are looking for any movement on the water, a blurb, blister, blight in the vastness of blue. Any imperfection may signal a fish or—angler's dream—an entire school.

I am not good at this. My eyesight is poor in the dim light of morning, and my concentration falls victim to the mesmerizing sparkle of endless water. My thoughts wander until I can't remember what I'm thinking.

"Three o'clock," David whispers.

Startled into action, I cast. An amateur arc of line floats through the air and plops into the nervous water, just short of its mark. I jiggle the rod anyway, wait. Nothing. It is so quiet we can hear the running of the current. I reel in.

David poles us a little closer to the mangroves. I bait his hook with a plump and squirmy shrimp. With one arm, he sidecasts between two spindly roots. Perfect. A bit intimidated, I try to do the same. Not bad, the cast. We wait. The water is quiet. Gorgeous.

We spend most of the morning this way, running from Sands Key south to Adams Key and then Caesar Creek. Hunt, cast, wait, reel. But by lunch, we have nothing to show for it. It is not lost time, however. During the hunt, we spot a huge stingray as it glides past the skiff, a Portuguese man-of-war that on closer inspection turns out to be a clear plastic bag, brown sponges that look eerily like broken vases, and a crab sallying forth from its hole.

It is in the dignified quiet of these excursions that David and I have our most unusual conversations. One time, he was trying to teach me the feeding habits of local fish. The predators—such as tarpon, bonefish, snook, permit—are attracted to the flow of water and the glimmer of color. They react on instinct, occasionally going after agitators. Bait fish prefer the protection of the seagrasses, the seclusion of sandy bottoms. Theirs is a game of hide-and-seek, survival its prize. All, regardless of size or shape, seem to like color, movement, sparkle, scent.

"Like men," I noted wryly.

David did not laugh.

Mostly, when we're out on the bay, we do not talk, especially if we're without the children. What we fish we throw back. We look, we point, we savor, we breathe in air that vacuums clean our lungs. Sometimes all that is more than enough.

Open Letter to My Son
(As He Leaves for College)

The realization came to me during that in-between time, the graying of day as it finally capitulates to night. You were walking across the baseball practice field with that familiar defiant gait, and the silhouette I saw framed against the sliding sun wasn't that of a little boy, the baby I once held in my arms, but of a young adult broadening in the shoulders and thickening about the neck. I knew then that you, my oldest son, were growing up to be a man, and I wasn't quite sure what that meant for me. I'm still not, except . . . except that in growing up, you've also grown away, stretched just beyond my reach so that you are one minute in my arms and the next somewhere I cannot go. Then again, isn't that the way it should be? A mother's goal should be to eventually make parenting obsolete—or at least almost so.

That late winter dusk, you were thirteen years old. Thirteen going on thirty. Your father had died two months earlier, and the pain of that loss, coupled with the sudden knowledge that I could lose you, too—lose in the figurative sense, of course, but to something I had as little control over—gripped my heart so sharply that I closed my eyes and rested my head on the steering wheel of our ancient Chevrolet van. You found me like that, remember?

"What's wrong?" you gasped. Your voice was still deciding on the octave it would rest.

"Nothing, nothing," I said quickly, though my chest was about to explode. An awkward silence followed; we both knew I was lying but neither of us intended to say anything about it. Then reality, the saving grace: "Kick the clay off your cleats, will you?"

You gave up baseball the following year. Said it was too painful to play. Reminded you too much of your father. I was disappointed, but you were already past the age where you listened to everything—or anything—your mother said. I remember, though, when you did.

Now you are off to a world of rathskellers and fraternities and dorms and study halls. Soon we'll know how well I've taught you—and how much you have learned. It's a strange thing, this growing up. Knowing it has to happen does not lighten the heaviness—or excitement—in my heart. I don't know whether to cry or clap.

Though I have tried, I can't tell you how to lead your life. But I can show you what I've done with mine. I've been fortunate to make my passion my work. I hope you'll be lucky enough to do the same, to discover that one of the greatest pleasures is the joy of working at something you love. Find a job that makes you greet the morning with a smile. Don't do something solely for money, or because I expect you to, or because you can't think of anything else you want. And for godsakes, don't do it because you'll get to wear Armani suits.

I've spent more time on work than on almost anything else. (You will, too.) But more than a means of income, my job as a writer has turned out to be an avenue of escape. You must know, of course, that it was my writing—an insatiable need to set into words emotion and experience—that sustained me after your father's death. Yet, I've met too many people who hated their jobs, and nothing strikes me as more pitiful than toiling away without a sense of mission. *Bo-oring.*

This advice comes with a caveat: Don't overdo it. There is a time for work and a time for play, and each in moderation. You come from a long, tireless line of workaholics, of men (until my generation, that is) who wrested their identity solely from the work they did. They enjoyed little else. I've tried not to let that happen to me.

Which leads me to the next point. Remember how you would roll your eyes whenever you caught me talking to my houseplants, watering them with fertilizer or spraying them with my homemade insecticide concoction? I wasn't doing it for the green foliage and the lush flowers that my ministrations would produce. I was doing it for *me*. Those plants were my Prozac, the balm for frazzled nerves. They were also my silent but adoring audience. When I was trimming back the yellowing leaves or repotting the ivy, I was also indulging myself in fantasy. This was when I dreamed—and dreamed big. This was when I challenged niggling fear, when I made the improbable possible, when I stripped away all the excuses to not try something. This was also when I plotted and planned.

May you find a refuge of this kind. If not gardening, then take up fishing, or woodworking—any activity you can do by yourself. Chances are you will spend some portion of your life alone, and enjoying a solitary endeavor may turn out to provide you with as much solace as pleasure.

You have always been a cautious child, and events have made you more so. As a boy learning to swim, you would balance yourself on the edge of the pool and look solemnly at the vast blue fabric of the water. No jumping in for you, no. I always had to coax you in. Believe me, that was a relief. Caution is a good thing, especially in youth, but you must also temper it with risk, *calculated* risk. Success comes to those willing to step beyond their comfort zone. Every time I send material to a publisher, I feel like I am jumping into that backyard pool of your childhood, unsure of how far I can swim. Sometimes I swim as gracefully as a champion—and wow, aren't I something! Other times I can barely dog-paddle fast enough to keep my head above water, and the embarrassment of all that flailing is bitter indeed. Yet, defeat is a most brilliant instructor. What's more, the most important lesson failure has taught me is this: Always, *always,* believe in yourself. Son, you have the power to make things happen. Sure, success requires a modicum of luck and timing. I won't lie to you and say those things don't count. But why fret over factors you can't control? Talent is good, but just as important are self-confidence and desire, the willingness to jump in head first. I hope I have transmitted that courage to you.

Granted, things won't always go your way no matter how much you try. You may, on occasion, think you are doomed, jinxed, condemned to a fate you don't deserve. Remember those batting slumps you suffered through? Awful, but they didn't last forever, did they? So, don't pity yourself. Don't make excuses for bad judgment or play the role of victim. It's sad to see how our society increasingly allows people to blame their problems on bad genes, repressed memories, original sin, social injustice, and Jerry Springer talk shows. Yes, life isn't fair, and yes, some guys seem to have all the luck. So? Get over it, and get to work.

And my, you have lots of work—and partying—ahead of you. College is the foyer to adulthood. It will introduce you to the responsibilities and privileges of grownups without having to pay for either. This is where you will begin to figure out who you want to be, what you want to do, where you want to go. (Finance or accounting? Graduate school or job? Pizza or sub?) In the process of choosing, do not forget the importance of family. We are home and haven, bank and bridge, guide and guardian, the one true source of companionship and support. Some of your happiest moments—and admittedly some of your worst, too—will come at the hands of people linked to you by blood or marriage. We'll be around before your first paycheck and long after your roommate has moved out.

I have been blessed with the devotion of two good men, your father and your stepfather. Maybe you've been taking notes and learning. I would like something just as wonderful for you. Find a partner for life, and pick her carefully, very carefully. (Preferably after you're out of school.) I know this is an old-fashioned idea in a time when people are divorcing more, marrying less, and choosing instead to live together. But, you are an old-fashioned boy raised by an old-fashioned mother. A good spouse is a blessing from God, and marriage, a job and sacrament. (In the meantime, always use a condom. Better still, practice abstinence. Sex is too beautiful a gift and too wonderful a pleasure to squander willy-nilly.)

Now, before I send you off into the big, bright world, I can't resist the temptation to tell you to:

- Make your bed everyday. It'll impress your dates.
- Buy two alarm clocks, one to nudge you awake, the other to keep you from going back to sleep. I won't be around to scream and shake you.
- Take classes with intriguing titles. It may be the only time you'll get a chance to learn about the Tiahuanaco Indians in Bolivia or the sexual habits of lemurs in the tropics.
- Read extensively, across geographical and cultural boundaries. It is the cheapest form of travel.
- Care for your body. Don't do drugs or drink. Exercise religiously. Middle age—a mere hop in the timeline, believe me—will be easier if you're good to yourself early.
- Don't use foul language. It's a sign of a weak imagination.
- Treat women as you would have men treat me.
- Watch your manners and your grooming. You don't need money to be a class act.
- Volunteer. Become politically active. Advocate for the needy. You are part of a community that needs you.
- Say your bedtime prayers nightly. God is never farther than a thought away.
- Buy things on sale, and look for value—high quality items at a fair price. I'd be delighted to supply you with your own monogrammed scissors for clipping coupons.
- Call home, and call often, and not always for a reason. Call just to say hello.
- Remind yourself about the wonder of life. I do this almost every morning by reading a lovely piece of wisdom on the inside leather cover of my tattered agenda book. It's from the Talmud: "A

person will be called upon to account on Judgment Day for every permissible thing he might have enjoyed but did not."

It's a wonderful world out there, son. Make it better.

Moving Up, Moving On

The brown-and-tan For Sale sign went up on the small swath of
lawn in front of my mother-in-law's duplex the other day. In the
brisk winds that precede summer's daily thunderstorms, it flaps
noisily as if wanting to make a statement. Kad-dpp, Kad-dpp, the
sign groans. I think it wants to flee its rusty hinges, but the man
from the real-estate office assures me that, barring hurricane-force
winds, it will not fly off like a lost soul. To secure the sign, he hammered a long wooden stake through the grass, down through the
soil, into the hard oolite. He drove the stake right into my past, un-
wittingly dividing the before from the now, the once was from the
never again.

My children inherited this small, coral-colored duplex from their
grandmother. Eight months later, I put it on the market. It was like
placing a piece of my life on the auction block. For more than a
decade, that duplex and, in particular, my mother-in-law in that duplex remained a physical connection to a life I had long stopped
living. The decision to sell—in a symbolic way, to sever that connection—was as much about business as it was about moving on. I
grew up five blocks from the duplex where my first husband was
raised, just across Northwest Seventh Street in Grapeland Heights,

in a house that was as unpretentious as a sleeping child. When we first moved into 811, I was in second grade and the house was a simple three-bedroom, one-bath stucco with no porch but a back-yard large enough to accommodate growth. The rooms were small, the carpet musty, and the kitchen a dark hole. My mother loved it. Though we lived in other houses during my childhood, in other cities, in other countries, we always returned to this one. Everything else was temporary, but 811, with my grandparents firmly ensconced in it, was home.

We were the first Cuban family to move onto this block of blue-collar, middle-class respectability, the first to speak Spanish, the first to put a religious statue on the lawn. But soon after we settled in, another Cuban family moved to Northwest Thirtieth Court. Then it was as though The Plague had arrived. For Sale signs went up: *Los americanos* began to move out. It would take a few more years for my old neighborhood to become completely Hispanic, a few years before hardware became *ferretería,* jewelry store *joyería,* and grocery *bodega.* Actually, it took my entire childhood; the process was that gradual but inevitable. And truth is, not everyone moved out. Mrs. Claussen, our next-door neighbor, remained in her two-bedroom house until she died. She had no family, and her closest friends were members of her Protestant church. So, she stayed. Occasionally, she traded plant cuttings with my grandmother, a wordless exchange that looked a lot like a game of charades. I also have photographs of her at our Christmas lunches, at my bridal shower, at my wedding, a blue-eyed, gray-haired lady in flower-print dresses, a Connecticut Yankee in King Arturo's court.

Because we were in the thick of this change, we paid it no heed. Instead, my family concentrated on another kind of transformation. To the old house, we added room air conditioners, which, to save money, could be used only in the evenings—but hey, what a luxury! In the living room, two red crushed-velvet sofas were placed around a coffee table and a framed print of the Sacred Heart of Jesus was hung on the wall. In the built-in bookcase of the dining room, my mother exhibited her mismatched glassware and china.

Fruit trees were planted in back and rose bushes in front, rimming the pedestal of my mother's white plaster statue of La Virgen de la Caridad del Cobre, Our Lady of Charity, Cuba's patron saint. Initially, my brother, sister, and I slept in one of the rooms, my parents in another, and my paternal grandparents in the third. On the winter nights the crickets sang too boisterously, I would crawl into bed with my sister to ward off the frightening noise. My grandmother would find me there in the morning, when she awakened me before dawn, before the other children, so I could swallow a concoction of yogurt and orange juice that she was sure would make me gain weight.

As the family grew, as the neighborhood evolved, so did the house. My grandfather, who worked in construction, built a bedroom beyond the jalousie-windowed Florida room. Later, another room and a bathroom were added on the side, but this last addition was so narrow we had to sit on the toilet sideways. That was just one of the house's many eccentricities. The back door, for instance, swelled when it rained, making it difficult to close, and there was one window in the children's room that tended to jam, so you always had to open it with help from the outside. During bad thunderstorms, the door to the attic clump-clumped ominously, which convinced me we were homesteading with ghosts. And the closets, oh the closets! They were so teeny-tiny, so dark, that it was a good thing we had few clothes to store. Still, this was home and we did not know better for a long, long time.

In the backyard, my grandfather eventually poured enough concrete to make a small, cement-floor patio to house a utility room with a washer—no more laundromats for my mother!—and he put up a basketball hoop, too. My brother, sister, and I played Horse, Around the World, and improvised box ball. We acquired a dog, a white-and-brown mutt one of my mother's co-workers at the shoe factory was giving away. We called her Mancha—Spot, in Spanish—and tried to teach her how to catch a ball and how to play dead. She learned to do neither, but she was a good pet anyway, jumping and wriggling and salivating whenever we returned home.

She never ate dog food because we didn't know anybody who fed dogs pre-packaged, store-bought meals. She lived instead quite happily, if unhealthily, on a steady diet of table scraps—everything from black beans and rice to chocolate ice cream. While my brother was allowed an occasional foray outside the yard to visit neighborhood boys, my sister and I rarely ventured beyond the chain-link gate, and it was on the cement patio that we learned to play patty cake in Spanish and to sing those childhood songs that nobody else in school could sing.

At recess, we chanted: Miss Lucy had a baby. She called him Tiny Tim. She put him in the bathtub to see if he could swim. At home, we countered: *Había una chinita sentada en un café, con los zapatos blancos y las medias al reves.* (A little Chinese girl sat at the cafe with her white shoes and her socks on backwards.) In school, Old Mc-Donald had a farm and on his farm he had a cow, a pig, a duck, a rooster, a cat, a dog, a horse. In our backyard, *el patio de mi casa es particular, llueve y se moja como los demás. Agáchate, niña, y vuelvete a agachar, que si no te agachas no sabes bailar.* (The patio at my house is special; it gets wet in the rain just like all the others. Bow down, girl, and bow down again, because if you don't we know you can't dance.) The morning's London Bridge game became the afternoon's *Al animo* and Ring Around the Rosy turned into *A la rueda rueda*. Already our world was dividing into two, and sometimes not in tidy halves.

So many years later, so many miles away, the words of these songs come back to me all at once, stumbling one over the other, eager to be heard. They're both familiar and strange, the chorus of another lifetime.

Arroz con leche se quiere casar con una viudita de la capital . . .
Había una vez un barquito chiquitico . . .
Ese lunar que tienes, cielito lindo, junto a la boca . . .
Naranja dulce, limón partido, dame un abraza que yo te pido . . .

I heard some of these songs the other day, in a school cafeteria where a poetry competition was being held. A husband-and-wife duo performed them on stage, trying to animate a sleepy crowd at 8:30 A.M. Like many of the other parents, I croaked along, clapping my hands while the children watched in amazement.

"How do you know those songs?" my youngest asked.

"I learned them a long time ago," I answered. Suddenly, briefly, I glimpsed the basketball hoop, the old dog, the chain-link fence, the hand-me-down clothes, the moving neighbors, the secret life and language of the cement patio. Between verses, I swallowed the lump in my throat.

After the show, I visited the singers' booth and forked over twenty-five dollars—on my platinum credit card, naturally—for their tapes, then I drove back with my Nike-shod, upper-income children to my suburban home with the ample closets and the huge, well-lighted kitchen and the doors that all close tight even when it rains. Sometimes, when I'm alone in the car, trapped in perennially horrible Miami traffic and too mentally exhausted to listen to anything as cerebral as NPR, I pop a tape in and sing along: *Los pollitos dicen pío, pío, pío, cuando tienen hambre, cuando tienen frío.* (The little chicks cry pio pio pio when they are hungry, when they are cold.)

The 'hood. That's what my children call the place their parents once thought of as home. There's a romantic and dangerous connotation to their words, an undercurrent of fascination with something so . . . so ethnic and vulnerable and different. The houses in Grapeland Heights are squat, boxy, interchangeably pastel colored, with black wrought-iron bars on windows and chain-link fences around yards. Religious statues—some in modest homemade chapels, others the size of a child—dot the landscape. Occasionally, you may discover a rusty old car resting on cement blocks, but by and large the driveways and pebbly swales are occupied by Ford Escorts and Chevrolet Cavaliers and Toyota Corollas, their sets of wheels complete. With rare exceptions, the streets are clean, the yards tended. There are sidewalks, barking dogs, skating children, ice-cream trucks. And always, always, people out and about, walking, going places. More than anything, it is the people and what they do with their time that differentiates my old neighborhood from the one I live in now, where people walk only for exercise and anything that must be bought—milk, bread, shoes, cough syrup, haircuts—is a good car drive away. In Grapeland Heights, there is still the feeling of city, of a community within hoofing distance. People shop at the Winn-Dixie or the Kmart on Thirty-seventh Avenue and haul their purchases home on two-wheeled carts. They sip *cafe* at open-air stands along Seventh Street and Flagler and leave bakeries with white boxes full of pastries and long, crusty loaves of Cuban bread. On street corners, vendors hawk *churros*, peeled oranges, *mamoncillos*. Weekends, during the off-season, neighbors flock to the flea market at the Flagler Dog Track, where you can buy anything from a potted ficus to a Seiko watch. Cash only.

It has changed, the 'hood. In the air, the smells and sounds are not what they were when we moved in or when we left. Though still a Cuban stronghold, the neighborhood is now home to many Central Americans, the singsong of their Spanish harmonizing with the Caribbean's quicker-paced, consonant-swallowing interpretation of the same language. The shops have changed, too—more video stores, more fast-food outlets, fewer mom-and-pop shops. An Avon distribution center has taken over the HUD office that once housed the old library where I learned to read English. The studio of a cable-TV channel has replaced the offices of a small, private school that went bankrupt. A restaurant is now an auto-parts store. One thing, however, remains the same: the blast and thunder of planes from nearby runways. I, all of us in the 'hood, grew up jowl to cheek with Miami International Airport and learned to live with the deafening boom of planes, which rattled windows and shook doors. The roar of jet engines—unpredictable, overwhelming, accepted—punctuated our conversations and forced us to time our phone calls, but we did not know different until we moved away.

And then, without looking back, without thinking twice, we adapted to the silence, to the empty streets, to the manicured rigidity of cookie-cutter development. Now, in the eerie quiet of suburban day, I am startled when I hear the faint rumble of engines overhead. I look away from my computer and out a window or door. I assure myself that the plane is a great and unfathomable distance away in the sky before returning to all these words, this strange and lovely English, on the screen.

The day I met the real-estate agent, I stopped at the bakery half a block from my old house. Once a rectangular hole-in-the-wall with scents to tempt the salivary glands, the shop has expanded its space and its offerings. Eclairs, *pasteles de guayaba, merengues, señoritas, flan, natilla,* and *pudín* still line the shelves of the refrigerated display case. But so do rows of *Tres Leches,* the delicious Nicaraguan dessert. Behind the cashier, fresh loaves of *pan cubano* are stacked beside plastic bags of large, saucer-shaped *galletas,* not far from a new cafeteria counter selling sandwiches and deli meats. I order a meat pastry and shot of coffee, then slowly drive north on my street. I want to compare my memory to reality. I figure yards will appear diminished, rose bushes faded, houses smaller. But no. My block is, mostly, as I remember. With the car idling, I loiter in front of 811, remembering all the times I dreamed about being somewhere else and realizing how, now that I am, I think not of returning but of the small, unappreciated moments that have accumulated to make me who I am. I inch down the length of two houses, to the alley that cuts through the street and leads to the elementary school. When I walked this route, egg yolk-colored allamanda crept along the chain-link fence, a riot of buds that seemed to blossom regardless of care or climate. It was the highlight of my walk to school, spotting those flowers on the vine, the one thing of beauty I saw before the expected day of anxiety in the classroom. Though a straight-A student, I never much liked school and reluctantly trudged there with my siblings, hoping to get it over with as quickly as possible.

I attended Kensington Park Elementary until the fourth grade, when my parents transferred us to the Catholic elementary school on the grounds of our parish church. Though I went to other schools, passed other grades, mastered many subjects, fourth grade remained a turning point in my life. It was 1965, the year of the civil-rights demonstrations in Selma and President Johnson's proposal for discussions to settle the Vietnam conflict. It was the year I learned that a threat is usually worse than reality, that an enemy can occasionally become an ally, and that there is no sweeter triumph than besting the person who tries to put you down.

Mrs. Scott wore her hair, the color of ebony, piled sternly atop her head in a perfectly shaped bun. She preferred shoes with square toes and sturdy heels, shoes people call sensible. And she had nothing in her wardrobe that would suggest the effervescence of spring. On most counts, she was an ideal fourth-grade teacher. She was not munificent with praise, but she was impeccably fair, if a little inflexible. She liked children who were respectful, who recited the Pledge of Allegiance without stumbling; girls who kept their nails clean and boys who did not run in the hall. Most of all, she liked children who spoke accentless English with the diction of Walter Cronkite. If one spoke Spanish, justice was meted out quickly. Such a transgression was akin to starting a fight. She pulled pupils by the thin hair of their sideburns into the principal's office or hit them across the knuckles with a long, wooden ruler. I toed the line.

"A good school citizen," she wrote in the back of my report card. "She is making good progress in arithmetic."

In spite of my progress in arithmetic, Mrs. Scott complained that I did not participate enough in class. This behavior was incomprehensible for my parents, who knew the timbre of my voice all too well, and at various loud ranges, too. Even my grandmother believed the teacher's farewell pat on my shoulder in the afternoons was a misplaced gesture, a case of mistaken identity. The little girl who attended school, demure and reserved, was not the same one she took home, rebellious and disrespectful.

"You save your real self for the house, eh?" she accused me, in the safety of the kitchen.

I snickered and threw my book bag across the table before walking away. From the Florida room, where my brother and sister were already quietly playing, I watched how she halved a tomato, mashed its juice on a slice of warm Cuban bread, and poured olive oil over it. Then she diced the shriveled remains onto the other slice. *Pan con tomate* was an after-school snack to be enjoyed alone, away from the curious stares of other children. I wolfed it down, resentful that the grown-ups knew nothing of the real world, my world. In school, after all, the code of behavior was different. We ate peas and applesauce, and the lilt of my voice, the way the R's rolled uncontrollably on my tongue, seemed as out of place as my grandmother's *pan con tomate*.

Maneuvering through those contrasts, keeping abreast of both worlds, was why every morning a nauseated feeling rose from the pit of my stomach, peaked in my esophagus, and broke at my throat. I refused to eat breakfast. Tearfully, I would rush to the bathroom and bend over the toilet. Nothing. I would try again, same results. So off to school I would go with a slice of lemon wrapped in wax paper. My grandmother said it would scare the vomit away. And, of course, a tart squirt to the base of the tongue always did. I was never without that wrapped lemon wedge.

One morning before the first bell rang, Doug discovered it in my hand. He was a stocky, towheaded boy with freckles and a chipped tooth. The class bully. I was deathly afraid of Doug because, until now, he had never bullied me, and so I was in a constant state of watchfulness, waiting, waiting, waiting. Finally, something was happening. Taunting, he showed the lemon wedge to all the other children, then squirted me in the eye. I whimpered. Everybody laughed, but Mrs. Scott caught him and hauled him to class by his sideburns. Later, practicing my cursive writing, I realized worrying about Doug had been wasted effort. A squirt to the eye was nothing. I also discovered that, without Mrs. Scott, I could have handled his bullying just fine because I was better than he was at something he liked. I was the fastest girl in the class and could run harder and better than some boys, including Doug. That day, heart at my throat, wind in my face, I ran home thinking of my secret treasures: the tomato sandwich, the yellow of the creeping alla-manda, my grandfather's cigar after dinner, the songs sung on the cement patio, my mother's steady hands when she sewed, my father's sleep-deepened voice in the morning.

I haven't been back to the school with its breezy halls and court-yard benches for almost ten years. Last time, I was there for Career Day. Mrs. Scott was long retired, maybe dead. There wasn't a tow-headed boy in the brown-haired bunch. And I knew I could not run a mile without panting, though I was making a good living with the language Mrs. Scott thought she protected. In the library—the media center, as they call it nowadays—the second graders watched expectantly as their teacher introduced me. I caught a phrase in Spanish, a language that sometimes sounds both painful and mel-lifluous to me. I began to tell them my story in this, my other lan-guage, and it rang deep, clear, accentless: a refugee's song.

Shifting gears in the car, I pull away from the alleyway and the running, from Doug and Mrs. Scott, and drive to the corner, turn west, and head for the expressway. Home.

For years, my second husband's father owned a crafts store not far from where my family lived, just down the block from St. Michael's Catholic Church, where I made my First Communion and married for the first time. David and I feel this has always been an unusual and ancient connection between us. Together, we can remember old restaurants, back streets, and what once was. A long time ago, in a reflective mood, I asked him if he believed the old adage that later became a jingle for a cigarette commercial of our youth. It stated, and I'm paraphrasing: You can take the boy out of the country, but you can't take the country out of the boy. We dis-cussed this but reached no conclusions. The past has passed, David likes to say. Or, That was a lifetime ago.

Every once in a while, he complains that I am a restless sleeper, stealing covers, nudging him to the edge of the bed, talking. There are nights, he adds, I mutter while I toss and turn, nights when there are as many words in our bedroom as stars in the heavens. What do I say? I ask him. Why am I carrying on so? He shrugs, then holds me. In those godless hours before daylight, he says I hold forth in Spanish. Sometimes, too, I sing.

5   6/09